Wallace-Homestead Price Guide to

AMERICAN *Country* ANTIQUES

11th EDITION

Wallace-Homestead
PRICE GUIDE TO

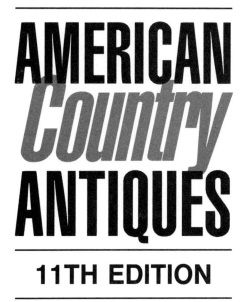

AMERICAN
ANTIQUES

11TH EDITION

Don & Carol Raycraft

Wallace-Homestead
Book Company
Radnor, Pennsylvania

This edition is dedicated
to the memory of our good friend,
Emmitt Holtzclaw,
of Lancaster, Kentucky

Library of Congress Catalog Card Number: 86-640023
ISBN 0-87069-616-5 *hardcover*
ISBN 0-87069-584-3 *paperback*

Designed by Anthony Jacobson
Cover photograph taken at Joseph & Peter Country Antiques,
   Berwyn, Pennsylvania
Manufactured in the United States of America

1 2 3 4 5 6 7 8 9 0   10 9 8 7 6 5 4 3 2 1

Contents

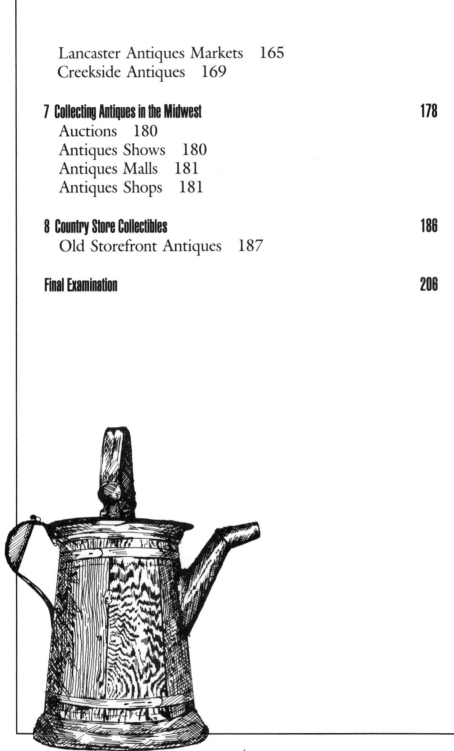

vi

Acknowledgments

Al Behr
Copake Country Auctions
Larry and Pat Coughlin
Country Village Antiques
Creekside Antiques
Ralph and Shirley Dukes
Teri and Joe Dziadul
Michael Fallon
Rose Holtzclaw
Alex Hood
James D. Julia Inc.

Joy and Robert Luke
Jim Martin
Patricia McDaniel
Pat Newsom
Old Sleepy Eye Club
Joe and Opal Pickens
Darrell and Lana Potter
Dawn and Randy Sprout
Ellen Tatem
Vicki and Bruce Wassdorp

Photography

Jon Balke
Al Behr
Ralph Dukes
Joe Dziadul
Tiffany Potter Fair
Mark Harper

Carol Raycraft
R. Craig Raycraft
Kyle C. Schiebel
Dawn Sprout
Ellen Tatem

Line Drawings

Melissa Strang

Introduction

Thomas Ormsbee, in his classic *Field Guide to Early American Antiques*, understood the price structure for Americana so well that more than forty years later his words are as timely and enlightening as when they were initially written.

> *As for value, prices for American antique furniture are not like those of standard commodities. They are determined individually and a number of factors are involved, such as age, rarity, design, craftsmanship, condition, and collector demand.*
>
> *On the other hand, there is a schedule of comparative values which is recognized and understood by experienced dealers and collectors. It applies year in and year out, with the ratios between the various price levels for different grades remaining fairly constant. Relative values for antiques of finer quality*

stay more or less the same through lean or boom years. Run-of-the-mill pieces are more readily affected. Their prices rise faster during inflation periods and decline with equal speed when a recession threatens.[1]

Contrary to what you may read in the antiques periodicals or hear at the flea market every Sunday in the American Legion parking lot, it is still possible to build a representative collection of Americana at reasonable prices if you take the time to consistently look in the right places. The truly *great* buys are found in the wrong places at the right time.

There are several exceptional pieces of stoneware illustrated and priced in the section on the Joy Luke Auction Gallery of Bloomington, Illinois. The gallery is located fifteen minutes from the scrubbed-top table on which this paragraph is being written.

On the day the Bennington stoneware crossed the auction block, we were 100 miles away at an "antiques" show sifting through booths filled with carnival glass, Coca-Cola bottles, and furniture that your Aunt Helen threw away in 1945 when Uncle Bill came home from the war. We were firm and practicing believers that little of consequence can be found within a ten-mile radius of your sock drawer. We were wrong.

We should have stayed at home and bought the stoneware.

How to Use the Prices in This Guide

The purpose of any price guide is to provide its readers with insights into the retail values of the items upon which it is focused.

We have attempted to accomplish that goal by securing pictures and prices from a variety of businesses spread geographically across the United States that are actively buying and/or selling Americana on a daily basis.

These sources include auction houses, antiques dealers, antiques cooperatives, and an antiques mall that specializes in country antiques.

We feel that this approach best reflects current market trends and accurately presents a fairly realistic portrait of the retail values of American country antiques.

It is important to always keep in mind that an item's actual value is determined only when a buyer and a seller reach an agreement about the worth of an object and a check is written.

A price guide should be used much like the catalogs produced by major auction galleries. The items in the catalog carry presale estimates of the value of items in the auction. The eventual selling price could be more or less, but the estimate of value provides a potential buyer with a better appreciation of the probable worth of the object. Most price guides should be perceived in the same manner.

---

[1]Thomas Ormsbee, *Field Guide to Early American Antiques* eighth ed. (Boston: Little, Brown, and Company, Inc., 1951).

We get a surprising number of letters and telephone calls over the course of a year from collectors who have questions about where they might go to find country antiques at "affordable" prices. You've heard it before—location is everything.

In this edition and in subsequent books, we will select an area of the United States that might be of special interest to antiques collectors looking for Americana and also provide information about shows, shops, malls, restaurants, and overnight accommodations in the vicinity that would enhance the visit.

We have chosen central Illinois for this initial effort because we are most familiar with it. In future editions we will call upon friends from throughout the nation whose opinions we respect to make additional recommendations.

We are *not* suggesting that you drive 2000 miles across America with pounding hearts to visit Central Illinois or any other place we mention. We *are* suggesting that a trip to the area would be an opportunity to see a significant amount of merchandise for sale in a relatively compact geographic area, and you undoubtedly will find some things to add to your collection at reasonable prices.

We feel it also is important that anything we recommend be accessible to families with children, priced competitively, and be readily available. There also should be some opportunities for experiences other than antiques hunting to make the expedition worthwhile.

The restaurants we list probably would not be discovered by a tourist passing through the area. They offer menus that are indigenous to the middle of Illinois and are well worth your time.

It is important that you schedule your trip around a weekend that highlights a major antiques event. This gives you the opportunity to see much more from which to select than at any other time.

The Third Sunday Market (May to September) at the McLean County Fairgrounds in Bloomington, Illinois, brings together more than 350 antiques dealers from Illinois, Indiana, Iowa, Missouri, and Wisconsin. Bloomington is located in the center of Illinois and is crisscrossed by several major interstate highways, including I-55, I-74, and I-39.

The Sunday Antiques Market (November and March) is an indoor version of the indoor-outdoor Third Sunday Market, with approximately 135 dealers converging upon the Red Bird Arena on the Illinois State University campus in Normal, Illinois (Bloomington's twin city).

Antiques Shows
Third Sunday Market
McLean County Fairgrounds
Rt. 9 (east)
(Third Sundays from May to
  September)
8–4 P.M.

Sunday Antiques Market
Red Bird Arena
Illinois State University
(November and March)
10–4:30 P.M.

Information:
P.O. Box 396
Bloomington, IL 61702–0396
(309) 452-7926

Antiques Malls

Chenoa Antiques Mall
Chenoa, IL 61726

Illinois Antiques Center
100 Walnut St.
Peoria, IL 61602

Pleasant Hill Antiques Mall
East Peoria, IL 61611

Auction Gallery

Joy Luke Gallery
300 E. Grove
Bloomington, IL 61702
(309) 828-5533

Restaurants

Charlie's Place
Kappa, Illinois
Thursday-Sunday
(309) 527-5518

The Village Inn
1115 Main Street
Minier, IL 61759
(309) 392-2327

Accommodations

Jumer's Chateau
1601 Jumer Drive
Bloomington, IL 61704
(309) 662-2020

Fairfield Inn by Marriott
202 Landmark Drive
Normal, IL 61761
(309) 454-6600
(800) 228-2800

Information About the Area

McLean County Chamber of
  Commerce
P.O. Box 1586
Bloomington, IL 61701
(309) 829-6344

Central Illinois Tourism Council
631 E. Washington Street
Springfield, IL 62701

Wallace-Homestead Price Guide to

AMERICAN *Country* ANTIQUES

11th EDITION

1 *Criteria for Buying Country Antiques*

It is difficult enough today to locate and purchase country antiques without adding some baggage to the equation, but for our purposes it is probably worthwhile.

Over the past twenty-five years, we have stumbled through basements in Bangor, attics in Altoona, and back porches in Peoria with flashlight in hand. Occasionally, we actually have uncovered something of minimal value that was for sale.

In recent years this process has slowed down as the attics have grown leaner and the demand for country antiques has become infinitely greater. Most of what we buy today is found at antiques shows and markets.

Here are a series of reasonably simple steps that a neophyte or veteran collector can utilize and appreciate to expedite the buying process and even save some money.

The price of any antique offered for sale by a dealer is a function of a multitude of variables. A selected few of these would include the cost of finding the item (gas, motels, meals, time, telephone); the purchase price of the item; overhead at shows and markets (booth or space rent, motels, food, telephone); profit margin (how much the seller has to make on the transaction); preparing the item to be sold (repair, refinish, refurbish, refine); and the attitude of the seller (how badly the seller wants to sell it).

Pricing Factors

The collector's mission is to make the purchase as economically as possible. To accomplish that goal there are some factors that should be pondered before the check is written.

Time of Show

The longer the dealer has been forced to look at a particular piece in his shop or at a show, the more likely it will be offered at a discount. A large cupboard on the first day of a two-day show may be priced at $2500 (dealer's cost: $1700). By 4 P.M. on the second day, with the show to close in thirty minutes, the dealer may be more disposed to reduce the price than lug the cupboard out the door, onto the truck, and back into the house or shop. If someone offers $2000, the odds are excellent they will have bought a cupboard.

Exceptions

When a dealer has a "good show" and sales have been brisk, the cupboard that didn't sell might not look as bad (or as heavy) at 4:30, and a significant discount probably would not be available.

It is not uncommon for a dealer to take a piece out of his or her own collection to "dress up" a booth at a show or market. The piece may be priced so high that only someone who *really* wants it will pay the price. It also serves as an enticement for customers to enter the booth and look at the other merchandise. The dealer doesn't really care if the piece sells in this situation.

Strategy

Obviously, the potential buyer who sees a cupboard on Saturday morning when the show opens is taking a major chance by gambling on coming back on Sunday at 4:15 in hopes it will still be there for a lesser price.

Attitude

For a transaction to take place, the seller and the customer each may want to have several "needs" fulfilled. The buyer must be convinced that the piece is fairly priced, within his or her budget, accurately described by the seller, and will fit into the room or specific space for which it is being purchased.

If the seller appears disinterested, hostile, or overly aggressive, the buyer may move on to the next booth or shop and the transaction never will be consummated.

The seller's attitude is a major factor in the selling process. The dealer should be well informed about the piece and price it accordingly. Any restoration or repair should be noted on the price tag. If the buyer asks questions, they should be answered informatively and politely. If the potential buyer inquires about a discount, the dealer should not be offended. The dealer should already have established a discount policy prior to opening his doors or unpacking his wares. There are *no* suggested retail prices for American antiques.

The buyer's attitude also can have a significant impact on the final price of a particular piece. The buyer should have some knowledge and not immediately offend the seller with negative comments about the piece.

If the buyer wants the piece, it should be purchased at that point without prolonged contemplation. On occasion customers have asked dealers to hold a piece for them until they have seen what else is being offered at the show. This ties up the dealer's merchandise unnecessarily. It is within the bounds for a customer to request an item to be "held" for fifteen to thirty minutes until a spouse arrives, a checkbook can be retrieved, or a telephone call can be made.

The dealer is not there to hear involved stories about previous successes or rare bargains from the past. The dealer wants to sell antiques.

Emotion

The buyer must walk an especially narrow line between abject disinterest and tears of joy when attempting to buy country antiques.

If it is obvious to the dealer that the customer absolutely cannot live without the item, the opportunity for discussion about the price is seriously compromised. The buyer should not get emotionally involved until after the check is written and the purchase is packed and the show or shop is in the rear view mirror.

Buying antiques is an emotional *and* intellectual process. It is important to keep each in the proper perspective.

The buyer should determine precisely what is being purchased (condition, finish, repairs, age) and the best possible price *before* beginning the final decision-making phase of the transaction.

Seller's Financial Condition

As noted previously, a dealer's success or lack of success is a mjaor determinant in the pricing of merchandise as the show winds down. The dealer has expenses including gas, booth rent, meals, motels, and time to recapture and needs to make sales.

The term "antiques show" is obviously deceptive because dealers are on hand to "sell" antiques and not "show" them. It is a great deal of work to prepare for an antique show or market. Items have to be priced, packed, loaded, set up, packed, loaded, and unloaded. It is a much simpler procedure to sell as much as possible at the show. Dealers are highly motivated to sell.

Markup

Contrary to popular opinion, most dealers do not have a "standard markup" on items they offer for sale. They do not attempt to have a similar profit margin on every item they sell. A department store usually can work on a predetermined profit margin, but an antiques dealer cannot.

If a dealer attends a rural auction in the rain on a cold March morning and buys a $750 (retail) painted pie safe for $75, the dealer would probably price the safe at $575 to $625 (wholesale) or $650 to $750 (retail) and be especially pleased with the profit margin.

At the same auction the dealer could become emotionally involved with a quilt and pay $225 for an item that will be difficult to sell for $250.

The quilt transaction may bring the dealer only a minimal profit, but the purchase of the pie safe made it a successful morning in the rain.

Dealers tend to price their items at prices they feel potential customers will pay. The goal is to be competitive *and* profitable. Many dealers sell a great deal of their merchandise to the trade (other dealers) at wholesale prices. The seller must leave "something" for the wholesale buyer, who also will attempt to sell the item at a profit.

In many areas a sales tax number is easier to obtain than a loaf of bread at a neighborhood convenience store. This creates a tremendous number of "dealers" who ask for trade discounts at shows.

Some collectors are convinced that dealers sometimes raise their prices when they do a show or market to cover additional expenses. Our experience has been that this is not normally the case. Most dealers offer their wares for the same price whether the transaction is taking place in a local shop or four hundred miles away at a weekend antiques show. It takes a significant amount of time and effort to reprice a boothful of merchandise.

Buyer's Primary Concerns

There are a series of questions that a potential buyer should ask about any purchase under consideration *before* the transaction is finalized.

How much is it?

Can I afford it?

Is it a "good buy"?

How am I going to get it home?

If I ever had to sell it, who am I going to call?

Do I have a place to put it?

Will it fit?

Am I going to have to sell something else to get it in the house?

What is the provenance of the piece?
   Who owned it?
   Where did it come from originally?
   From whom did the dealer acquire it?

What is its structural condition?
   Any repairs?
      "new" repairs?
      "old" repairs?
      minor repairs?
      major repairs?
      quality of workmanship of the repairs?

What is the approximate age of the piece?

Is all the wear in the "right" places?

What about the surface of the piece?
   original painted surface?
   repainted or overpainted surface?
   "new" paint?
   stripped and refinished?
   stripped and unfinished?
   "skinned"?
   original, unpainted surface?
   "as found" condition?

How about the price?
   Is the piece
      the last of the great bargains?
      affordable?
      underpriced?
      overpriced?
      greatly overpriced?

What is the difference between the asking price *and the* selling price?

What is the best price *the dealer will take?*

Is there a discount for cash?

Will the dealer take a check?

Is delivery available? If so, is there a charge?

Will the dealer provide a receipt that in-

cludes his or her name, address, and telephone number; a description of the piece (age and surface); notation of any repairs; provenance if known; date of sale; and the selling price and applicable tax?

Condition

When you have finally found the piece of country furniture that you can afford, you are certain that it will fit precisely where you want it, and you have a way to get it home and two guys that will load it into the back of a pickup truck, pause for a moment. Determine in your mind which of the definitions from the following list that your purchase matches.

1. "as found" or "in the rough"
2. completely original
3. fake
4. "married"
5. reproduction
6. restored

A piece that is "as found" or "in the rough" has just emerged from fifty years on a back porch; a century in the hayloft or barn; or from your brother-in-law's garage, where it was nestled next to your toolbox that he borrowed three years ago.

A piece that is as found normally presents few surprises. Seldom has an attempt been made to repair, refinish, or refurbish it before you had the chance to buy it. It may be filthy, devoid of a door, and missing its hinges. However, in most instances, it is what it appears to be.

It is very difficult to find a piece of country furniture that predates 1900 that can accurately be described as "completely original." To fall within that category the piece must come out of the house exactly the same as it went into it a century or more before. The

finish, hardware, and glass must be original to the piece. There can be no structural deletions or additions. If a cupboard has been stripped or over-painted, it is obviously not completely original.

The major difference between a "fake" and a "reproduction" is the intent of the maker. A fake is made to fool a potential buyer into writing a check for something that is not what it is alleged to be. It can be made from "old" wood, be held together by eighteenth-century handwrought iron nails, and have a $3500 price tag—but it still is not an antique.

A reproduction is a piece of furniture made to resemble an antique. The maker, seller, and buyer all understand this. It is not unusual for a reproduction to combine several distinct styles or periods into a single piece.

Initially, most reproductions are marked or "signed" by the manufacturer or individual craftsman to give some indication of its point of origin. It is important to understand that furniture has been reproduced individually and in quantity for five hundred years.

A piece of furniture that is "married" may give the appearance of being completely original, but that can be a potentially costly and false impression. A marriage is consummated when the doors of a cupboard purchased in pieces at a farm auction are coupled with a cupboard that has everything but its original doors. The paint or finish is matched and the cupboard is now complete and appears to be original.

The base of a two-piece pine cupboard that lost its top a generation ago can be married to a pine hanging cupboard and have its value multiplied several times.

The degree or percentage of restoration and its effect on the value of country furniture is a hotly contested issue. Few collectors expect to find completely original examples of nineteenth-century furniture that have survived to the present without a replaced piece of molding, new hinges or door pulls, or a reconstructed foot.

The potential buyer should request detailed information about the restoration to hardware, paint, finish, and any structural changes. As mentioned previously, this should be noted on the receipt of the purchased item.

2 *Kitchen and Hearth Antiques*

This chapter was prepared by Teri and Joe Dziadul and it illustrates items from their personal collection. The Dziaduls have been filling special requests for more than twenty years and offer kitchen and hearth antiques for sale to collectors and dealers. The current list may be obtained by sending $1 to:
Teri and Joe Dziadul
6 South George Washington Road
Enfield, CT 06082

In colonial times homes were poorly heated and ventilated. As Benjamin Franklin remarked of those who sat before the roaring fire in the main room on a winter night, "They scorched before and frooze behind."

Cotton Mather, shivering in the winter of 1697 before such a "great fire," noted that "Juices forced out of the end of short billets of wood by the heat of the flame on which they were laid, yet froze into Ice on their coming out."

From early histories collectors of kitchen and hearth accessories will find articles to appreciate the social living in those periods. Here in New England early homes are saltbox houses in quiet village settings or weathered shingled cottages along the coast.

The settlers invented dishes which have become cherished traditions. Clam chowder was eaten at the beginning of the week. Toward the end of the week leftovers made a platter of "red flannel" hash. The hash was colored by beets and eaten with sour milk biscuits, applesauce sprinkled with nutmeg and dotted with butter, and a custard so light it hardly counted.

Codfish cakes and balls reigned at the Sunday breakfast table, and dinnertime yielded the traditional pork and beans which had been in the beehive oven since early Saturday.

After sundown, with the Sabbath over, the kitchen was apple fragrant with the aroma of yellow-green pound sweets as Mother cut them, still baking hot, into bowls of johnny cake and milk.

With the day's cooking accomplished and the fire burning low, children could sit on the bob-hob, a stone projection seat built into the brick side wall. If the night was clear, one could look right up the chimney and see the twinkling stars. If a storm raged outside, snow or rain spattered on the embers in the fireplace. The expression "hob-nobbing" with so-and-so probably arose from sharing such a seat in the fireplace.

The present-day collector, consumed with childhood memories, is creating an impact in the antiques market for nostalgic memorabilia. Ice cream scoops, apple peelers, whipping devices and egg beaters are much sought after.

There are conflicting opinions on this "middle market." Our experience leans heavily toward a prosperous, growing demand in this area. In spite of a cool economy, examples of the very finest in all categories still command escalating prices.

Painted and decorated box with black background, mustard yellow and red decoration, and "MEDICINES" painted on the cover. **$675–$775**

Sponged decoration wooden box with brown and mustard yellow sponged design, early construction, and original lock closure. **$775–$875**

Small painted watering can, most likely for a child, painted red with floral design. **$225–$275**

1864 sampler, **$675–$875**; painted bride's box, **$1500–$1800**.

Samplers were created in countless tiny cross-stitches by most girls in the New World. Each girl worked on her sampler daily and learned not only embroidery, but also spelling, Biblical verses, and rhymes. The diligence then expected of children is revealed to us complete to the last, often crooked letter. Shown is a typical bentwood bride's box with a design of the bride and the groom amid floral and emblematic decorations.

Tin barrel in scarce form with tin construction. **$795–$895**

Punched tin coffeepot from Berks County, Pennsylvania, in punched tulip design. **$875–$975**

Dutch oven for down-hearth cooking. Coals were heaped below and on top of the lid for cooking. **$475–$500**

Iron kettle. **$275–$295**

Large iron kettles were used outdoors and hung on a tripod over an open fire. They were employed for tasks such as making soap, boiling down sap, and washing clothes.

Iron shovel, "Pat. Union Fork and Hoe, pat. 1926," **$25–$30**; wrought-iron footman used near the hearth for resting kettles, plates, and pans, eighteenth century, **$425–$495**; cast-iron kettle, eighteenth century, **$250–$295.**

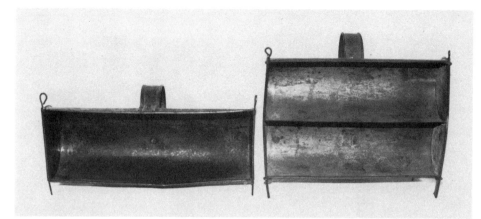

Tin apple roasters in single-shelf and double-shelf versions. **$450–$550**

When in his sixties, Mark Twain wrote, "I know the look of an apple that is roasting and sizzling on a hearth on a winter's evening and I know the comfort that comes of eating it hot, along with some sugar and a drench of cream...."

Tin bird roasters with pivoting hoods to check on the progress of roasting birds. **$245–$295**

Tin bird roaster with wire hooks for hanging small game birds to roast on the heart. **$195–$225**

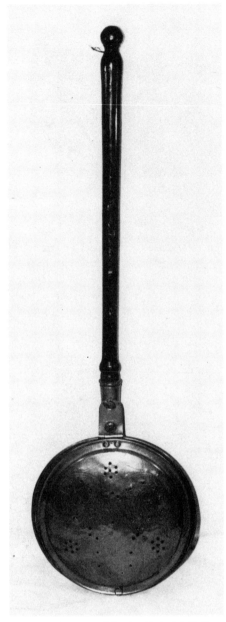

Wrought-iron cressets like this one were used at the hearth to hold hard pine knots for light. **$525–$575**

Bed-warming pan (Martha Dziadul Collection) with pierced brass lid and wooden handle. **$350–$395**

Coals were put in the pan and slid between bone-chilling bed coverings to warm them.

Hot coals were placed in the inner tin box of this all-wood foot warmer to warm feet in cold weather. **$450–$495**

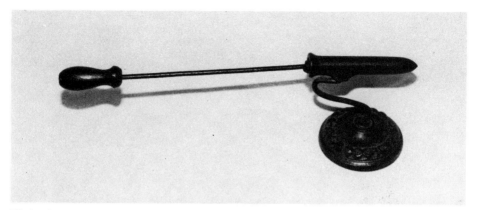

Diminutive gophering iron marked "Kenrick," with faint remnants of original gold finish and decorative floral border, $2\frac{7}{8}''$ in diameter, $3\frac{7}{8}''$ high. **$195–$225**

Tin candle molds: 6 tube with stretcher base, **$295–$325**; 12 tube that is longer than most molds, **$175–$195**; 12 tube with wire ring holder, **$225–$275.**

Church candle box measuring $18\frac{1}{2}''$ long. **$195–$225**

Unlike most tin candle boxes, which hung on the wall near the hearth, this is a flat-bottomed holder which came from a church in Pennsylvania. There is no handle or hasp closure.

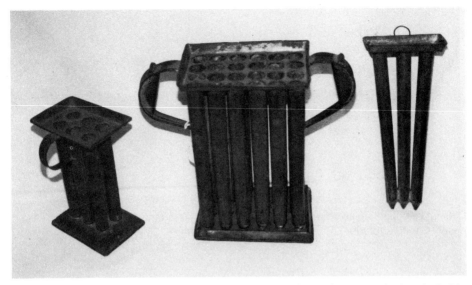

Tin candle molds: 6 tube for $6\frac{1}{2}''$ candle (uncommon size), **$250–$295**; 24 tube in a desirable size, **$275–$295**; 3 tube splayed and soldered at the wick end, **$175–$195**.

Push-up hogscraper candlesticks: $9\frac{1}{2}''$ high, marked "Dowler, 1751–1808," **$625–$695**; $7\frac{1}{2}''$ high, marked "Dowler, 1751–1808," **$275–$295**; $5\frac{1}{4}''$ high, marked "Shaw," **$300–$375**

Mounted wood lemon squeezer, **$225–$275**; silver glass lemon reamer, **$95–$110**; wood lemon reamer, **$150–$185**.

In 1768, John Crosby of Boston, "Lemon Trader near the sign of the Lime," offered fresh lemons at 12 shillings per dozen.

Flour sifter (Rosella Tinsley Collection) with iron sifting paddles, c. 1840. **$300–$350**

Wrought-iron kettle lamp with trunnion mount. The central wick support eliminates the problem of drip; early nineteenth century. **$550–$595**

17

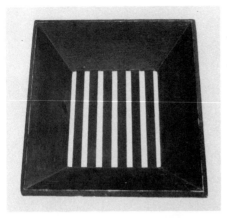

Wood cheese drainer with original red paint. **$575–$650**

Wood flour sifter (Rosella Tinsley Collection) in scarce version from mid-nineteenth century. **$395–$450**

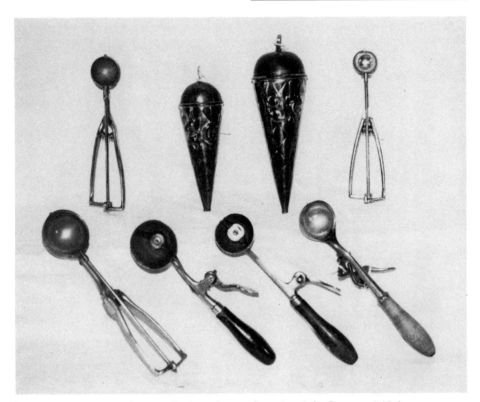

Ice cream scoops and cone display pieces, from top left: Bonzer #40 brass scoop, **$120–$135;** brass ice cream parlor display, waffle design, embossed "2¢," **$265–$295;** brass ice cream parlor display, waffle design, embossed "3¢," **$355–$395;** Ergos brass sherbet scoop, **$120–$135;** Bronzer 3 oz. brass scoop, **$110–$120;** Gilchrist, 10, rare form, **$195–$225;** Gilchrist, 12, rare form, **$195–$225;** Trojan, Troy, N.Y., **$110–$125.**

Ice cream lick glasses, **$65–$85;** chrome scoop, **$45–$50.**

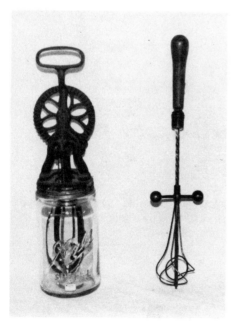

Whippers and beaters: Holt's Improved iron mayonnaise mixer-beater, pat. by Holt-Lyon Co. Beater apparatus affixed to Ball special glass jar, **$175–$195;** Archimedes' screw principle action beater, **$195–$225.**

Raisin seeders (Rosella Tinsley Collection): Crown raisin seeder, pat. Oct. 26, 1896, **$95–$110**; EZY raisin seeder, pat. May 21, 1895, **$225–$295.**

The Union cast-iron apple peeler, Nov. 11, 1866. **$185–$210**

Shaker all-wood apple peeler with attached knife, clamps onto table or bench. **$775–$895**

Improved Baystate 64 cast-iron apple peeler, made by Goodell Co., double table clamp. **$165–$185**

Cast-iron peelers: Turntable '98 made by Goodell Co. of Antrim, N.H., pat. May 24, 1898, **$95–$110;** Oriole, "Scott Mfr. Co. Balt. Pat. Pend.," **$300–$350.**

Cast-iron peelers and segmenter: clamp-on apple segmenter, "Pat. Feb. 1, 1869," a mechanical device to quarter or segment an apple, **$425–$475;** peach peeler, "Sinclair Scott Co. Baltimore, made in USA," **$120–$140;** "S.S. Hersey, Pat. June 18, '61 and Aug. 30," **$195–$225.**

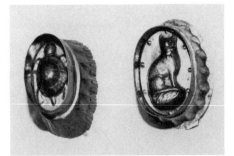

Tin food molds (Rosella Tinsley Collection): all-tin turtle design, **$125–$150;** tin-skirted copper cat design, **$150–$195.**

Pair of tin cookie cutters, man and woman, 14½″ high. **$650–$750**

In early account books of tinsmiths, cookie cutters were entered as cake cutters. Indeed, many were as thick as cakes.

Tin food mold (Rosella Tinsley Collection) with tin skirt and copper lion design. **$175–$195**

Tall man cookie cutter, 18″ high. **$650–$750**

The early cutters are cut close to the form of the design, with little or no tin to spare.

Cookie cutters: pitcher, **$150–$175**; horse, **$125–$145**.

Household utensils were the mainstay of the tinsmith's trade. However, cookie cutters in pitcher form were not very common.

Man driving car cookie cutter, almost 16″ long. **$1200–$1400**

This cookie cutter would produce a great amount of detail. *Lebkuchen,* a thick, chewy cookie, was a favorite Christmas cookie. Ginger and molasses were key ingredients in this popular holiday cookie.

Jockey on horse cookie cutter, 13½″ long. **$625–$695**

Tinsmiths expressed wide imagination in their creations. They would cater to their customers' special requests as well.

23

Large cookie cutters: 19½″ long jockey on horse, **$1600–$1800**; man on bicycle, **$1200–$1400**

Eagle butter mold and stamps: case mold, **$400–$450**; rare lollipop stamp, **$1200–$1400**; half round stamp, **$875–$975.**

Springerle boards: rare Father Christmas design, **$200–$250;** marked "Germany," **$75–$95;** intricate carving and interesting subjects, **$175–$200.**

Eagle butter stamp. **$675–$975**

Butter stamps and molds: apple butter stamp, **$95–$125**; apple case mold, **$150–$175**; strawberries stamp, **$200–$275**; pear stamp, **$175–$200**.

Butter stamps: stylized rose, **$175–$240**; rose, **$200–$250**; basket of flowers, **$375–$450**; stylized lily, **$300–$375**.

Cow butter stamps. **$375–$450**

26

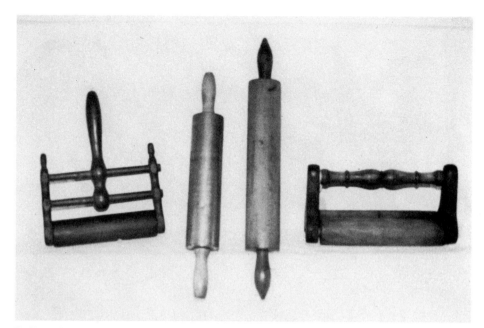

Rolling pins: eighteenth-century double bar, **$425–$495**; tin rolling pin, **$300–$395**; rolling pin attributed to Shakers, **$95–$125**; rare chestnut and maple double rolling pin, **$450–$500**.

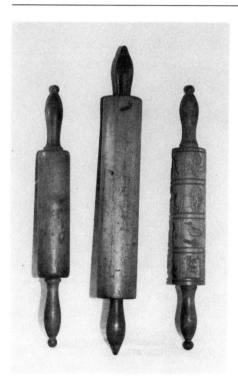

Wood crimping board and roller featuring moistened, starched fabric rolled on a board to crimp ruffles. **$275–$295**

Wood rolling pins: maple with turned handles, **$35–$40**; Shaker rolling pin, **$95–$125**; Springerle rolling pin, **$175–$20**.

27

Apple tea caddy, **$2500–$2800**; pear tea caddy, **$1600–$1800.**

Tea caddies were lined with tinfoil and outfitted with locks (when tea was so precious and expensive) and made from fruitwoods such as apple.

Catalogs: The Spice Mill, May 1921, advertisers of coffees, teas, spices, extracts, etc., **$25–$30**; Talbot, Brooks, and Ayer Household Utensils, **$25–$30.**

Wood salt boxes: painted green and red, **$275–$325**; rare miniature salt box, **$125–$175.**

Herb crushers: eighteenth-century iron crusher, **$850–$1000;** wood herb crusher, **$500–$600.**

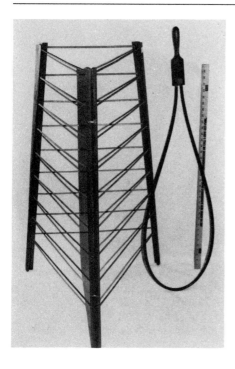

Shaker herb drying rack, **$325–$395;** Bentwood beater with green paper label "Hancock Shakers, Mass.," 42½″ long, **$235–$275.**

Nutmeg graters: wood bottle form, **$375–$475**; coquilla nut carving on base, **$350–$395**; fruitwood pear, **$625–$695**.

Mechanical nutmeg graters: tin and wood, "The Common Sense," **$450–$495**; cast iron, marked "Domestic Nutmeg Grater," **$550–$650**.

Cinnamon grater, scarce, **$525–$575**; wood pocket grater, **$550–$595**.

Nutmeg graters: handmade and painted, **$275–$300**; tin on wood frame, **$120–$130**.

Mechanical nutmeg grater made of wood and brass, Champion Grater Co., Boston, Mass., pat. 1866. **$475–$525**

Nutmeg graters: Tin with teardrop form, top lid has grating surface, lower lid lifts for nutmeg storage, embossed heart within heart design, **$550–$600;** embossed flower with tole painting, **$550–$600.**

Tin pocket nutmeg graters in oval and ellipitcal form. **$175–$195**

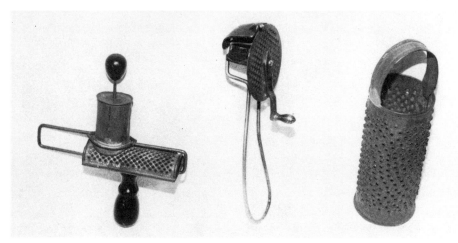

Nutmeg graters: the Edgar, **$125–$175;** wire handle, **$175–$250;** hand-punched grater, **$75–$85.**

Wood spice chest with porcelain drawer labels and porcelain rosette knobs. **$250–$295**

Tin spice set in carrier with gold japanning and red and blue painted tin. **$175–$225**

Wood spice chest with brass scroll labels. **$395–$450**

Spice chest and spice tower (Martha Dziadul Doak Collection): wood spice chest, black stenciled drawer labels, c. 1875, **$375–$395**; four-tier spice tower, paper scroll labels, c. 1820, **$395–$450**.

Shaker sewing box lined with brown silk and outfitted with needle case, pincushion, and emery. **$495–$550**

Wood pails: painted green with paper label, **$175–$195**; Shaker, painted red, **$350–$395**.

Splint basket with deep kick-up bottom construction, unusual metal ears, wire handle with wood grip, c. 1860. **$325–$375**

Miniature splint baskets with more intricate weaving and form are more desirable. **$175–$295**

Nantucket baskets: round, **$1100–$1200;** oval, **$1200–$1400;** signed "Sylvaro, Orange St. Nantucket, Mass.," **$1400–$1600.**

Many baskets were made on the *No. 1 Lightship,* Nantucket, New South Shoal, which was 24 miles south of Santaky Light in 1856. In a constricted space, ten isolated people, with little to do but clean lamps and stand watch, made some of the finest baskets. Marked examples have the highest value.

Doris Stauble arrangement of fruits and old millinery material in a sponge bowl. **$250–$295**

Doris Stauble arrangement of mohair squirrel and millinery materials in an old wood box. **$275–$295**

Doris Stauble arrangement of wax fruits and millinery material in old splint basket. **$295–$325**

Doris Stauble lamp featuring wood fruit, bird, and old millinery material in punched-tin basket. **$400–$475**

Curtiss Chicos spanish peanuts jar mounted in the tin frame with tin cover, large country store dispenser. **$425–$475**

Blown glass storage jars: $16\frac{1}{2}''$ high, scarce size, **$295–$350;** $12\frac{1}{2}''$ high, blown applied rings, **$250–$295;** $14\frac{1}{2}''$ high, blown applied rings, **$250–$295.**

Pedestal cake stand, **$55–$85;** silk apple pincushions, **$55–$95.**

Cake stand. **$95–$125**

Popular during the Victorian era, stands like this proudly displayed creative cakes and tarts.

Christmas candle lights, from top left: blown cobalt, **$85–$95;** ruby light, **$150–$175;** light with tin base, **$85–$95;** aqua pressed leaf pattern, **$75–$85;** bottom row of blown-into-mold lights in clear, amber, amethyst, sea green, cobalt, **$20–$25** each.

Plate warmer. **$675–$795**

The plate warmer is open at one side, which faces the fire. A door at the back enables plates to be easily put in and taken out.

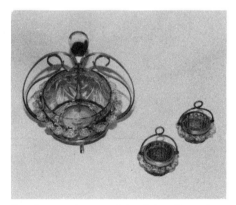

Cranberry glass: relish dish, silver-plate holder, applied rigaree, **$125–$175;** salt dips, silver-plate frame, applied rigaree, **$85–$95.**

Make-dos: goblet, **$175–$195**; engraved goblet, **$175–$225**; Sandwich glass whale oil lamp, **$200–$225**; lamp, **$175–$195**.

Royal Doulton silver-plated jar, **$275–$295**; wire biscuit pricker, **$85–$95**; wood biscuit pricker and stamp which reads "innocense" [sic] and carved sheep, **$450–$495**.

Glass storage jars with tin lids: blown into mold, dated 1856, **$95–$110**; tall storage jar, 11″ high, **$110–$125**; blown into mold, brown asphaltum finish on lid, **$95–$110**.

Cheese dish by Franz Mehlen, blue and white covered dish, c. 1850. **$225–$275**

Turkey platter and 8 dinner plates from Cauldon, England, flow blue and white. **$850–$950** set

Chinese export china mug make-do, a superb example with classic wrought-iron handle, c. 1760. **$325–$395**

Delft platter, 16″ diameter, signed "Delft," mid-nineteenth century. **$775–$875**

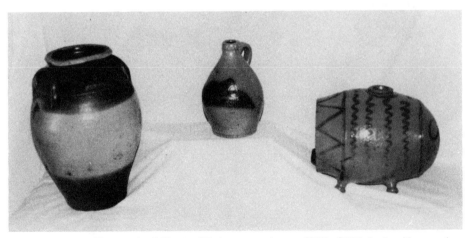

Stoneware: eared jug marked "Boston" in brown and gray, **$250–$300;** incised beaver jug with cobalt decoration, **$1800–$2000;** blind pig cooler, **$695–$895.**

40

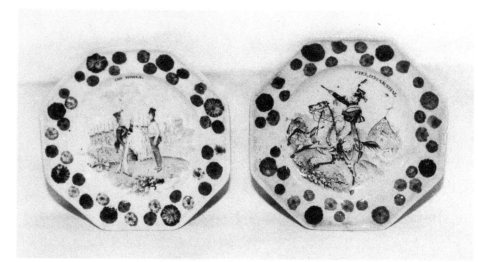

Soft paste cup plates with military themes and red and green painted decoration. **$175–$200** each

Merchant's stoneware jug with cobalt script. **$275–$295**

Soft paste cup plates from top left: Brown and Mulberry Staffordshire plates, **$125–$145;** flow blue, Davenport, **$115–$125;** Blue Willow, **$75–$85.**

Prior to the mid-1850s, hot tea was sipped from saucers rather than the cup. The handleless cup, being too hot to hold, was put on a cup plate.

41

Brown and cream covered crocks in 1-to-3-gallon set. **$250–$295**

Stoneware crock with bird and floral cobalt decoration. **$800–$895**

Large stoneware crock. **$550–$595**

Wood footstool with early mortised construction. **$125–$175**

Wood bread boards: "Be Thankful," **$145–$195;** "Give Us This Day Our Daily Bread," **$175–$225.**

Dummy boards, also referred to as silent companions, c. 1800. **$2500–$2800** pair

Child's pull toy locomotive in wood with all original red and black paint. **$2200–$2500**

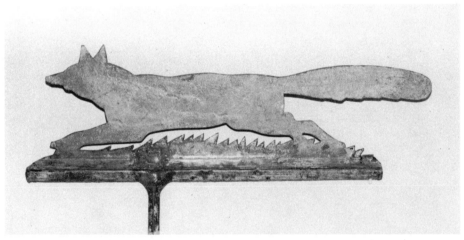

Sheet metal weathervane in running fox form, reflecting the sport of country gentry. **$675–$875**

To the ancient Greeks (who invented the weathervane) and the Romans, the winds had personalities. Vanes were oracles of good or bad times, not just wind direction indicators. The use of weathervanes decreased in the late nineteenth century as Americans moved toward an urban society.

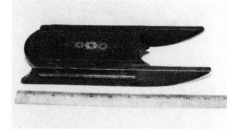

Miniature sled with red paint and floral decoration. **$275–$300**

Doll's settle and rocker painted red with gilded decoration. Settle, **$85–$95;** rocking chair, **$110–$125.**

Child's stove outfitted with tin utensils. Stove has red, black, and gold paint. **$200–$225**

45

3 *Americana at Auction*

Copake Country Auctions

Michael Fallon is an auctioneer and appraiser who conducts cataloged Americana auction sales of formal and country furniture, Shaker, quilts, coverlets, hooked rugs, samplers, and folk art. He is a member of the National Association of Certified Auctioneers, National Auctioneers Association, New England Appraisers Association, International Society of Appraisers, and the Columbia County Chamber of Commerce.

The items that follow have sold recently at the Copake Country Auctions. Mr. Fallon may be contacted at:

Mr. Michael Fallon
Copake Country Auctions
Box H
Copake, NY 12516
(518) 329-1142

Eighteenth-century fireside chair, **$1900;** Jenny Lind bureau set, **$475;** eighteenth-century New York State chest, **$775.**

Eighteenth-century Rhode Island Queen Anne drop-leaf table. **$3000**

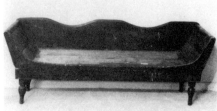

Early nineteenth-century settee. **$400**

Cast-iron bench. **$1200**

Pennsylvania tall chest, cherry, c. 1810, **$1100;** tiger maple Queen Anne highboy, c. 1750, **$9150.**

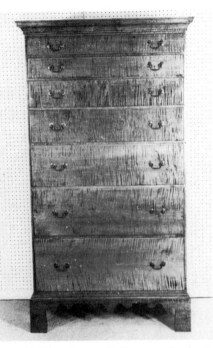

Twentieth-century solid tiger maple chest-on-frame. **$2970**

Portrait of a gentleman, **$575**; decorated tole box, **$350**; two-drawer tiger maple and cherry stand, **$1800.**

Walnut Sheraton server from the Delaware Valley, c. 1810. **$1650**

Clockwise from top left: sled, **$300–$350**; blue bowl, **$400–$500**; Steiff dog, **$700–$900**; bucket, **$250–$275**; Shaker's seed box, **$300–$400**; red chest, **$575–$675**; Gardner seed box, **$375–$425**.

Stack of painted pantry boxes, c. 1880s. **$225–$275** each

Blue painted candle lantern, c. 1900. **$300–$375**

Oak splint basket, c. early 1900s. **$200–$275**

Cast-iron wheeled coffee grinder with original painted finish, c. late 1800s. **$600–$775**

Collection of nineteenth-century cobalt-decorated stoneware. **$200–$600** each

Cast-iron "Mogul" windmill weight, c. early 1900s. **$1600–$2200**

"Rainbow tail" windmill weight from Elgin, Illinois, c. early 1900s. **$1200–$1400**

Cast-iron rooster windmill weight from Elgin, Illinois, c. early 1900s. **$900–$1300**

Steiff dog, c. early 1900s. **$700–$900**

Birdhouse found in Vermont, c. 1920. **$125–$140**

Painted storage house for garden tools, 40″ × 24″ × 30″, c. 1900. **$600–$700**

Painted firkins, c. late 1800s. **$275–$350** each

Three painted rocking chairs, c. 1870–1880. **$225–$300** each

Zinc-lined storage humidor for cigars, c. late 1800s. **$500–$800**

General Woodhull drop-leaf table. **$900**

Small Baltimore server with some restoration. **$1650**

Eighteenth-century maple Queen Anne lowboy. **$2200**

Decorated blanket box from Schoharie County, N.Y. **$4950**

American walnut Davenport desk. **$750**

Tramp art fireplace mantle. **$1650**

Oak file, **$450**; oak roll-top desk, **$2200**; two-door oak cabinet, **$175**.

French bread cupboard, **$175**; country secretary-desk, **$375**.

Early New England grain-painted 36″ slant-lid desk. **$5500**

Exceptional nineteenth-century cupboard, original "grungy" red paint. **$385**

Two-door Canadian cupboard. **$425**

Canadian pewter cupboard. **$2600**

Irish early nineteenth-century clock, **$2000**; Pennsylvania corner cupboard, **$2400**.

Storage cupboard, **$575**; Diamond Dye cabinet, **$550**.

Folk art clock signed and dated "1919," 16" tall. **$1650**

Janis Price painting deaccessioned from the Museum of American Folk Art. **$350**

Whaling off Labrador, oil on canvas. **$775**

Anonymous nineteenth-century allegorical scene deaccessioned from the Museum of American Folk Art. **$2850**

Rita Schroeder painting deaccessioned from the Museum of American Folk Art. **$775**

Portrait from New York State. **$1000**

Pat Thomas painting *Washington Park,* deaccessioned from the Museum of American Folk Art. **$400**

Fritz Vogt pencil drawing. **$4150**

Baltimore. **$1450**

Residence of Mr. Steven Hide, Chestnut Street, South Hadley, Mass., 1891. **$400**

Giles family record, Groton, Mass., 1825. **$700**

Pennsylvania bookplate, "Jacob Ungene 1815." **$2000**

Silhouette of Chauncey Goodrich, a professor at Yale University, and Mrs. Goodrich, daughter of Noah Webster, signed "Aug. Edwart 1841." **$1000**

Silk embroidered memorial "Lydia Gladding, Providence, Rhode Island, 1809." **$1800**

Folky shadowbox diorama. **$400**

Trompe l'oeil signed "JFP." **$3750**

Miniature portrait of an American sea captain. **$825**

Miniature primitive painting. **$2200**

Pennsylvania fraktur, Mt. Pleasant, rare Hebrew script. **$4675**

Reading toy boat model. **$220**

Hooked rug. **$800**

Sampler appliqué quilt, Poughkeepsie, N.Y., c. 1880. **$1550**

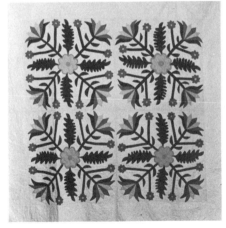

Appliqué quilt. **$1000**

Sunshine and Shadows Amish quilt. **$850**

"Lone Star" quilt, **$800**; Adirondack five-piece furniture set, **$800.**

Diamond sawtooth in square quilt, dated 1920 and initialed. **$700**

Complex log cabin quilt. **$1550**

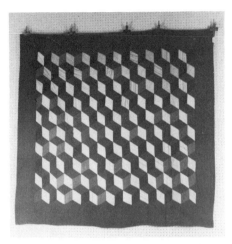

Pennsylvania "tumbling blocks" quilt. **$475**

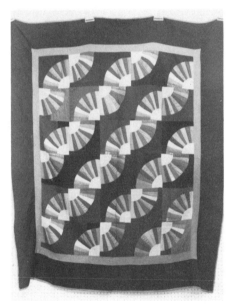

Amish fans quilt by Mrs. Eli Bontraeger, signed and dated, "as found" condition, deaccessioned from the Museum of American Folk Art, 1935. **$475**

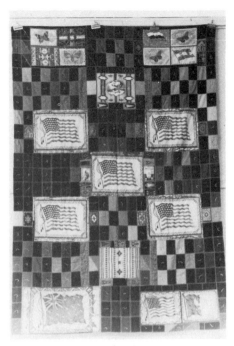

Flag quilt, c. 1919. **$450**

Pennsylvania "lighting" log cabin quilt. **$660**

Tole-decorated coffeepot, **$200;** and syrup, **$275.**

Silk quilt. **$440**

Mt. Lebanon, N.Y., collection of Shaker herb labels. **$450**

Recruiting poster, litho on canvas. **$100**

Carved French Gothic wooden Christ figure. **$400**

Carved by Jarvis Boone, Sugar Loaf Mountain, N.Y., c. 1940–1950. **$350**

James Robedee folk art carving. **$850**

Canada goose decoy, Barnegat Bay, N.J.
$225

Pennsylvania bird tree, 13½″ tall. **$1100**

Victorian witch puppet. **$300**

Early wood horse weathervane with sheet metal tail. **$3950**

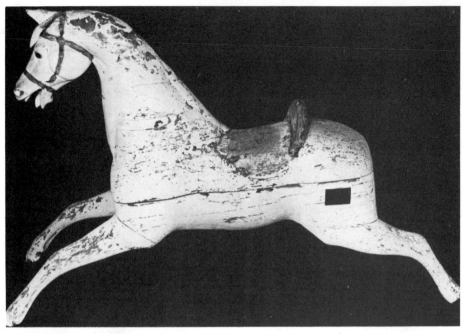

Carousel horse. **$1375**

Large twig birdhouse. **$350**

Carved wooden rooster weathervane. **$1500**

66

Wright Brothers whirligig. **$2450**

Whirligig in mint condition, c. 1930. **$450**

Sailor whirligig, St. Michael's, Md. **$1450**

Dime store clown used in window displays, c. 1940s. **$250**

Joy Luke Auction Gallery

The Joy Luke Auction Gallery is an auction and appraisal company that conducts estate and consignment catalogued auctions and specialized sales through the year. They feature estate jewelry, Indian artifacts, dolls, toys, textiles, and furniture. The Joy Luke auctioneers are members of the National Auctioneers Association and the Illinois State Auctioneers Association.

Joy Luke's commission is 20 percent, and all items are fully insured. Catalogs, mailing lists, and additional information may be secured by contacting:

Joy Luke Auction Gallery
300 E. Grove Street
Bloomington, IL 61702
(309) 828-5533

Pine pie safe with pierced tin sides and door panels and drawer at base, 61″ high, 38″ wide. **$670**

Early pine washing bench with two shelves and one storage cupboard at the base, refinished, 52″ high, 26″ wide. **$400**

Spinning wheel, **$250**; Chainomatic Christian Becker scale, **$200**; oak mixed-wood kitchen cupboard-dry sink, 78″ high, 49″ wide, **$400.**

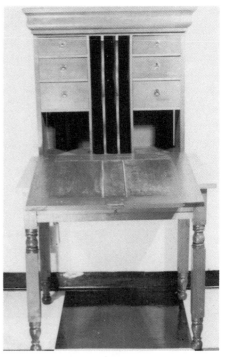

Cherry drop-front desk with six small interior drawers. **$550**

Early pine step-back cupboard with glazed doors and storage area below, 85" high, 44" wide. **$350**

Early walnut step-back China cupboard with glazed doors. **$1500**

Walnut corner cupboard with two glass doors and two paneled lower drawers, 87" high, 53" wide. **$2100**

Victorian walnut and burlwood cylinder roll secretary-bookcase, 98" high, 45" wide. **$2000**

Mahogany dental cabinet made by the American Cabinet Company. **$650**

Sewing table with ornately carved pedestal base. **$550**

Early mixed-wood cabinet with lift top and ten drawers, refinished. **$210**

Victorian and burlwood bedroom set featuring high-back bed, dresser with high-back mirror, and washstand with marble top. **$3050**

Oak blanket chest with lower drawer and claw feet. **$1250**

Flow blue bowl decorated with boat and windmill marked "Limoge," **$50;** flow blue plate with Kyber pattern, **$90;** flow blue teapot with pewter lid and copper base, **$250.**

Mettlach pottery humidor with raised decoration of cows. **$425**

Early cup, saucer, and two plates in Madras pattern. **$40**

73

"Three Guardsmen" tobacco jar, **$100;** Noritake tobacco jar with bulldog, **$350;** Limoges humidor, "Come Take a Smoke with Me," **$130.**

Blue and white ironstone Hanover Place cake plate. **$80**

Cameo glass vase with simulated tortoise-shell decoration and incised signature "LeVerre Francais." **$1800**

Large blue and white Minton jardiniere. **$350**

Custard glass table set with Maple Leaf pattern. **$450**

Blue custard glass table set in Chrysanthemum Sprig pattern. **$750**

Handel humidor featuring two owls in branches. **$500**

Limoges porcelain jardiniere decorated with flowers and elephant head handles with a separate base. **$250**

Mary Gregory figures are featured on these glass pieces. Pair of green glass tumblers decorated with a boy and girl, **$150;** pair of cranberry glass tumblers ornamented with a boy and girl, **$100;** cranberry glass tumbler featuring a girl, **$40;** pink overlay glass vase decorated with a girl and hoop, **$150.**

Decorated satin glass pickle jar in Albany silver-plated stand, **$375;** decorated glass pickle jar, Amberina Thumbprint pattern, in Rogers Bros. stand, **$400;** decorated cranberry glass to clear pickle jar, Thumbprint pattern, Rogers silver-plated stand, **$325.**

Double pickle jar decorated with storks in ornate, silver-plated stand, **$425;** olive jar with pit holder in Meridan stand, **$350.**

Coronet Limoges porcelain plate. **$40**

Decorated Amberina jam jar with silver-plated lid and handle, **$350;** decorated Amberina pickle jar with Thumbprint pattern in Pairpoint silver-plated stand, **$500.**

Majolica leaf plate in shades of green, brown, pink, and white, 11″ long, **$65;** Majolica plate decorated with birds and hollyberries, 11¼″ long, **$55.**

Tiffany toothpick holder in iridescent gold with dimpled sides, signed "L.C.T." **$225**

Collection of dolls and Victorian painted sled. **$625**

Group of iron painted Santas, left to right: **$140, $120, $100, $180, $155.**

Early toy rocking horse with original paint. **$400**

Victorian two-story dollhouse with porch and balcony. **$350**

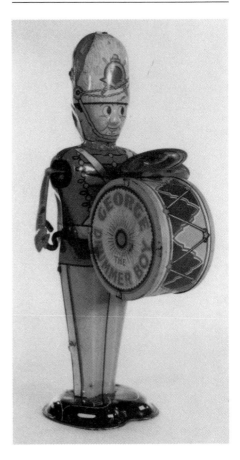

Marx tin wind-up toy, "George the Drummer Boy." **$200**

Shoenhut toys: elephant, **$225**; bareback rider, **$250**; brown horse, **$110**; bareback rider, **$300.**

Lionel GGI Engine #2332, black with five stripes, marked "Pennsylvania," excellent condition with the original box. **$1300**

Lionel 1950 Hudson Steam Engine #773, 4-6-4 with tender #2426W, marked "Lionel Lines," like-new condition with original box for the engine. **$1400**

Lionel standard gauge "Blue Comet" train set in excellent condition. **$2400**

Lionel gray Hudson steam engine and gray coal tender marked "Lionel Lines," in excellent condition with original boxes. **$2500**

Rare Lionel girl's train set with pink steam engine, excellent condition with original boxes. **$5000**

Lionel "Hiawatha" train set, restored to like-new condition. **$1075**

Lionel GGI steam engine and coal tender, engine not in running condition but otherwise in excellent condition with original boxes. **$1350**

Lionel GGI engine, maroon with five stripes, marked "Pennsylvania," excellent condition with original box. **$1500**

Small Regina disc music box in wooden case with 11″ disc. **$1050**

Polyphone disc music box with simulated rosewood case with thirteen discs. **$1000**

Swiss "Imperial Symphonia" coin-operated disc music box with mahogany case and six 15" discs. **$1800**

Swiss cylinder music box with bells, butter-fly, and birds; plays ten tunes. **$1200**

German wood case wall clock. **$400**

Early 1900s postcard album. **$80**

Jerome rosewood veneer shelf clock with glass door. **$30**

Swiss perpetual calendar pocket watch with enamel face, Roman numerals, month, day, date, second sweep hand and moon phase. **$450**

Gilbert oak case shelf clock. **$150**

President of the United States Zachary Taylor's 18 kt. gold pocket watch. **$3000**

Early double-wheel coffee grinder signed "Fairbanks, Morse and Company, Chicago." **$175**

Early spinning wheel, refinished. **$400**

Large oval lidded wicker basket. **$60**

Refinished maple and pine Boston rocking chair, c. mid-nineteenth century. **$275**

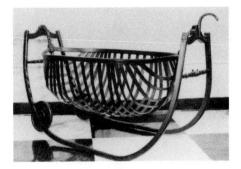

Swinging bentwood cradle. **$350**

James D. Julia, Inc.

James D. Julia Inc. conducts periodic auctions of Americana, glassware, waterfowl decoys and bird carvings, lamps, firearms, and country store and advertising items. Their catalogs are lavishly illustrated and highly descriptive of the items to be sold. Information may be secured by contacting:

James D. Julia, Inc.
P.O. Box 830
Fairfield, ME 04937
(207) 453-7904

The photographs that follow are from an Americana auction held on August 23, 1989, in Rockport, Maine.

Early Maine country one-piece open-top corner cupboard, old grey over mustard inside, red over old grey outside (red outside is not antique). **$1400**

Two-piece country Hepplewhite secretary, stripped down to old red and tan interior. **$1750**

Diminutive eighteenth-century Queen Anne flattop highboy. **$10,800**

Small pewter coffeepot or teapot, **$275;** eighteenth-century Queen Anne candle stand, **$2050.**

Paint-decorated dome-top storage box with bold red paint and black spotted decoration, **$750;** small early eighteenth-century Queen Anne blanket chest with old red paint, **$3250.**

Paint-decorated two-door cupboard with two drawers at bottom and turned feet. **$4250**

Late eighteenth-century poplar scroll-top corner cupboard. **$10,250**

Paint-decorated dome-top storage box with brown and yellow sponge decoration, **$450;** Queen Anne eighteenth-century blanket chest with dark old red paint, **$1800.**

Two-tier wall box, natural finish with scalloped top, old patina. **$450**

Collection of nineteenth-century decorated stoneware pottery (top row): **$100, $95, $250**; (middle row): **$650, $100, $350, $225**; (bottom row): **$850, $110, $1900**.

Fine Queen Anne slant-front bracket-base desk, old refinish. **$5000**

From top left: five-gallon crock, singing bird on a stump, **$425**; very rare large incised ovoid crock, **$2250**; rare three-gallon jug stamped "J. & E. Norton, Bennington, Vt.," **$4500**; ovoid decorated jug stamped "Lyman and Clark, Gardiner, Maine," **$550**; two-gallon jug with cobalt singing bird on a branch, **$300**; large stoneware batter pitcher, Fort Edward, N.Y., **$275**; one-gallon batter crock with blue cobalt floral decoration, **$1375**.

Collection of redware pottery. **$65–$225** each

Collection of eight baskets (top): round splint gathering basket, **$150;** (middle row): double swing-handled basket, **$550;** covered rectangular splint storage basket, **$150;** splint bulbous-shaped covered handled basket, **$120;** (bottom row): splint open-weave hexagonal handled basket, **$100;** rectangular Indian splint gathering basket, **$60;** small round splint egg gathering basket, **$350;** splint swing-handled basket, 11″ × 15″, **$400.**

Six decorated storage baskets from Maine with original covers (top to bottom): **$350, $125, $250, $250, $225, $150.**

Pair of folk-carved and painted figures of gentleman (16″ tall) and lady (14½″ tall), c. 1870s. **$4000** pair

Running horse wooden weathervane, 48″.
$3750

Collection of eleven butter prints, stamps, and a one-pound square butter mold (top row left to right): **$70, $225, $950, $25, $175;** (bottom row left to right): **$200, $80, $125, $90, $100, $100.**

Shaker-type oval boxes (top to bottom): one-fingered box in apple red paint, $5\frac{1}{2}″$, **$275;** one-fingered box in worn blue paint, $6\frac{1}{2}″$, **$325;** one-fingered box in worn grey paint, $7\frac{1}{2}″$, **$100;** two-fingered box, refinished, $8\frac{1}{4}″$, **$225;** large oval box with three fingers, natural finish with no paint, 12″, **$350;** very large oval box with four finely worked fingers, natural patina, $13\frac{1}{2}″$, **$750.**

Early toy locomotive, **$700;** tin ladder truck with iron wheels, "Pat. April 21, 1908," **$400;** cast-iron ladder wagon with three horses, **$500.**

4 *Decorated Stoneware*

Most casual collectors of American decorated stoneware are primarily concerned with the amount of "blue" that a piece carries and its price tag. Serious collectors evaluate stoneware on the basis of its decoration, maker, condition, form, and cost.

Unlike most examples of Americana, stoneware usually can be dated with surprising accuracy by the potter's mark impressed into the piece. For example, a three-gallon jug marked "E. and L. P. Norton, Bennington, Vermont" was made between 1861 and 1881 because that branch of the Norton family operated the business during that period of time. Other pottery marks may have been used for only a year or two before the pottery was destroyed by fire, bankruptcy, or the merger of several local potteries into a larger operation.

The four-gallon crock signed "Fort Edward Pottery Co." has a slip-trailed scene that includes a deer, stump, and ground cover.

Examples of decorated American stoneware with people are extremely rare.

The slip-trailed fish is signed "A. O. Whitmore, Havana, N.Y."

Most birds that have been slip-trailed or brushed on stoneware contain bits and pieces from robins, blue birds, chickens, hawks, and eagles. Rarely was a bird depicted as it actually appeared in the wild or in the apple tree in the backyard.

Three-gallon crock with brushed cobalt flower and impressed capacity and maker's mark from Pittston, Pa.

Stenciled decoration on a Cowden butter pail signed "F. H. Cowden, Harrisburg."

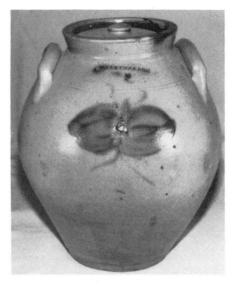

Ovoid two-gallon jar from Bennington, Vt., signed "Norton & Son."

Unmarked milk pitcher with brushed decoration.

Hundreds of potteries made and decorated utilitarian stoneware during the nineteenth century, from Maine to the Mississippi and beyond. Relatively few pieces have survived without some chips, cracks, nicks, pings, frys, and flaking because the pieces were made to be used. They were available in quantity, inexpensive, and difficult or impossible to repair if cracked or dropped.

Collectors should be concerned with much more than the amount of "blue" a piece may have.

97

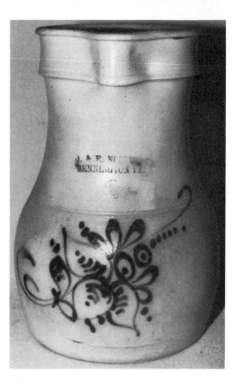

Slip-trailed two-gallon pitcher marked "J. & E. Norton, Bennington, Vt."

Evaluating Decorated Stoneware

In evaluating any piece of decorated stoneware pottery, it is crucial to consider the following factors.

Method of construction
  Thrown on a potter's wheel
  Molded

Damage
  Chips
  Flaking of cobalt decoration
  Stains
  Discoloration
  Pebble bursts
  Cracks
    Major
    Hairline
    Repaired
    Not repaired
    Quality of the repair

Decoration
  Type
    Swirls
    Number
    Geometric
    Flowers
    Birds
    Animals
    Humans
    Patriotic
    Scenes
  Size and detail of the decoration
    Overall proportion in relation to the size of the piece of pottery
  How the decoration was executed
    Incised or impressed
    Brush
    Slip cup
    Stencil
    Combination of brush and stencil
    Stamp

98

Maker of the piece	*Churn*
Signed or marked	*Jug*
Unsigned or not marked	*Jar*
Age of the piece	*Cooler*
1780–early 1800s	*Pitcher*
1820s–1840s	*Speciality pieces*
1850s–1870s	*Mugs*
1870s–1880s	*Batter pails*
1890–1920s	*Milk pans*
1930 to present	*Spittoons*
Color of the clay	*Flasks*
Type of stoneware piece	*Banks*
Crock	*Barrels*

The Wassdorp Collection

Vicki and Bruce Wassdorp have been in the antiques business for more than twenty years. They sell nineteenth-century Americana, furniture, and accessories in original condition. Much of their business is from the sale of decorated stoneware pottery. They publish a semiannual illustrated price list of stoneware for sale. A great deal of their stoneware business is conducted by mail with novice and advanced collectors and dealers from throughout the United States. Information may be secured by contacting:

Vicki and Bruce Wassdorp
10931 Main Street
Clarence, NY 14031
(716) 759-2361

As noted previously, the prices that follow should be perceived as a guide, similar to presale estimates of values at an auction.

Two-gallon jug signed "J. & E. Norton, Bennington, Vt." with detailed sitting deer decoration. **$4000**

99

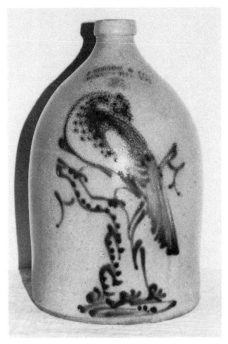

Two-gallon jug signed J. Norton & Co., Bennington, Vt." with detailed peacock on a stump. **$1800**

Three-gallon jug signed "F. Stetzenmeyer & Goetzman, Rochester, N.Y." with detailed and vivid floral decoration. **$1500**

Four- and three-gallon crocks signed "Burger & Co., Rochester, N.Y." with typical fern wreath decor with gallon size in middle. **$250–$550** each

Three-gallon jug signed "Whites, Utica," (N.Y.) with slip-decorated "running bird." **$650**

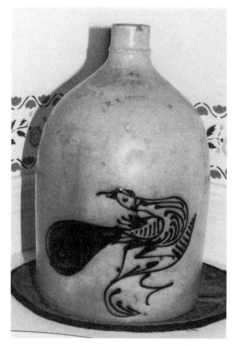

Two-gallon jug signed "N. A. White & Son, Utica, N.Y." with paddle-tail running bird decoration. **$650**

One-gallon straight-side crock signed "Whites, Utica," with slip-decorated running bird, **$450–$650;** one-gallon jug signed "Whites, Utica" with slip-decorated bird on a branch, **$500–$700.**

Six-gallon straight-sided crock signed "J. Norton & Co., Bennington, Vt." with vividly detailed slip-decorated floral spray. **$700**

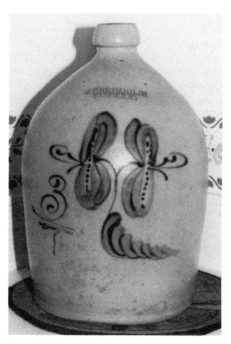

Three-gallon jug signed "J. Shepard, Jr., Geddes, N.Y." with stylized brush- and slip-decorated floral design. **$250–$500**

Two-gallon preserve jar with desirable "F. Stetzenmeyer, Rochester, N.Y." signature and well-detailed flower decoration. **$1500**

One-half gallon preserve jar, unmarked, attributed to Cortland, N.Y., with "2 quarts" in blue slip. **$250–$450**

Five-gallon crock, unsigned, with rare "chicken pecking corn" design. **$550–$950**

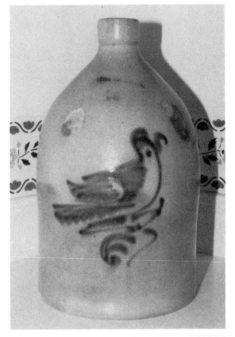

Two-gallon jug signed "Fort Edward, N.Y." with slip-decorated "fat" bird decoration. **$450–$650**

One-half gallon preserve jar, unmarked, attributed to Cortland, N.Y., in rare small size with slip decoration. **$250–$450**

One-half gallon jug, unmarked, attributed to Cortland, N.Y., with slip-decorated double floral design. **$350–$650**

Rare double-handled five-gallon jug with Seneca Falls, N.Y., store or vendor's mark, decorated with a large bird on a branch. **$900–$1400**

Three-gallon preserve jar signed "N. Clark & Co., Lyons" (N.Y.) with large brushed floral design and double "3" capacity marks. **$750–$1250**

Five-gallon straight-sided crock signed "N. Clark & Co., Lyons" with an extremely well-detailed large floral decoration. **$1500–$2500**

Two-gallon jug signed "Whites' Binghamton" with slip-decorated double floral design. **$250–$500**

Four-gallon straight-sided crock signed "A. O. Whitmore, Havana, N.Y." with very rare decoration of a house with double palm trees. **$3500–$4500**

Two-gallon preserve jar signed "J. A. & C. W. Underwood, Ft. Edward, N.Y." with slip-decorated bird on a branch. **$450–$650**

Four-gallon preserve jar signed "Harrington & Burger, Rochester" with slip-decorated double floral decoration. **$1500**

Three-gallon preserve jar signed "Harrington & Burger, Rochester" with slip-decorated double floral design. **$1200–$1500**

Two-gallon cream pot signed "Clark & Co., Lyons" with rare slip-decorated starburst design. **$2500**

Three-gallon ovoid jug signed "N. Clark, Rochester, N.Y." with vivid floral decoration. **$1500**

One-gallon jug signed "H. M. Whitman, Havana, N.Y." with rare slip-decorated fish. **$3500–$4500**

Two-gallon ovoid jug signed "John Burger, Rochester," with large slip-decorated daisy. **$600–$900**

Four-gallon straight-sided crock signed "Whites, Utica" with a rare slip-decorated running bird looking backward. **$650–$950**

Four-gallon cream pot signed "N. Clark & Co., Lyons" with a four-bud brushed floral decoration. **$750–$1250**

Two-gallon straight-sided crock signed "F. Stetzenmeyer & G. Goetzman, Rochester, N.Y." with large floral decoration. **$900**

Two-gallon straight-sided crock signed "N. A. White & Son, Utica, N.Y." with paddle-tail bird decoration. **$650**

Two-gallon preserve jar signed "J. & E. Norton, Bennington, Vt." with peacock on stump. **$800–$1200**

Two-gallon straight-sided crock signed "Whites, Utica" with slip-decorated running bird. **$650–$950**

Three-gallon ovoid crock signed "Clark & Fox, Athens" (N.Y.) with unusual "1832" date decoration. **$450–$950**

Four-gallon churn signed "John Burger, Rochester" with rare huge and detailed floral decoration. **$1800**

Five-gallon straight-sided crock signed "White & Co., Binghamton" with unusual folky house and tree—rare decorations. **$3500**

One-gallon milk or water pitcher signed "Lyons" with simple brushed clover flower design. **$750–$1450**

Two-gallon jug signed "J. Burger Jr., Rochester, N.Y." with wreath decoration and gallon size in center, **$250–$550**; two-gallon preserve jar signed "Penn Yan" with unusual slip-decorated framed floral design. **$550–$750**

One-gallon water pitcher signed "Burger & Lang, Rochester, N.Y." with double brush floral decoration. **$950–$1650**

Two-gallon jug signed "Burger & Lang, Rochester, N.Y." and dated "1872." **$450–$950**

Two-gallon preserve jar signed "J. E. & E. Norton, Bennington, Vt." with vividly detailed geometric floral decoration. **$650–$950**

Three one-gallon preserve jars, signed "Lyons," "Cortland," and "Penn Yan." All have brushed floral decorations. **$250–$550** each

Three-gallon jug signed "John Burger, Rochester," (N.Y.) with large floral decoration. **$650–$1150**

Two-gallon rare cake crock with slip-decorated plume signed "New York Stoneware Company, Fort Edward, N.Y.," **$350–$450**; three-gallon straight-sided crock signed "N. A. White & Son, Utica, N.Y." with bright blue orchid design, **$250–$500.**

Two-gallon preserve jar signed "N. Clark Jr., Athens, N.Y." with large fat bird decoration, **$550–$850**; two-gallon jug signed "N. White & Co., Binghamton" with poppy design in blue slip, **$250–$500.**

Three-gallon straight-sided crock signed "Burger & Co., Rochester, N.Y." with slip-decorated floral design. **$450–$900**

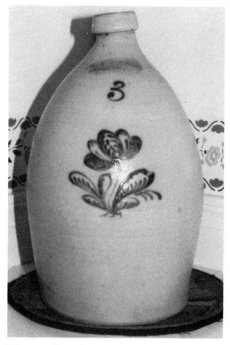

Three-gallon jug signed "John Burger, Rochester" with slip-decorated floral design. **$450–$900**

Four-gallon double-handled cooler signed "Cortland" with brush-decorated flower. **$1150–$1450**

One-half-gallon preserve jar with rare "Cortland" signature and slip- and brush-decorated flower, **$250–$550**; one-half-gallon unsigned preserve jar attributed to Whites, Binghamton, N.Y., decorated in blue slip, **$250–$550.**

Six-gallon straight-sided crock signed "C. W. Braun, Buffalo, N.Y." with brush- and slip-decorated double flower. **$450–$750**

Two-gallon jug signed "Geddes, N.Y." with top to bottom brushed flower decoration. **$450–$750.**

Two-gallon early ovoid jug signed "Seymour, Troy," (N.Y.) with early decoration of a simple brushed flower, **$300–$550;** two-gallon beehive-shaped jug from Ft. Edward, N.Y., with slip-trailed blue bird, **$450–$650.**

Two 2-gallon preserve jars from Lyons, N.Y., with brushed flower decoration. **$250–$450** each

Two-gallon straight-sided crock signed "J. Burger Jr., Rochester, N.Y." with slip-decorated fern, **$250–$550;** two-gallon straight-sided crock signed "Ottman Bros., Ft. Edward, N.Y." with fat bird decoration, **$400–$650.**

Two one-gallon preserve jars both signed "Lyons" with brush flower designs, **$250–$550** each; with a one-half-gallon unsigned advertising jug with the store mark "Dyer, Albany, N.Y.," **$150–$250.**

Two-gallon jug signed "Satterly and Mory, Ft. Edward, N.Y." with bird on a plume, **$450–$650;** two-gallon jug signed "Burger Bros. and Co., Rochester, N.Y." with slip-decorated flower, **$450–$900.**

Four-gallon cream pot signed "John Burger, Rochester" with vivid daisy design in blue slip, **$450–$900;** three-gallon straight-sided crock signed "Burger Bros. and Co., Rochester, N.Y." with slip-decorated two-bud flower design, **$250–$550.**

The Three Behrs Collection

The pictures of stoneware that follow are from the extensive collection of the Three Behrs. The Behrs have been sending out illustrated catalogs of stoneware that they have been selling for almost twenty years. They have sold stoneware by mail order to collectors and dealers throughout the United States. The Behrs also offer a lengthy list of stoneware-related books that can be ordered by mail.

The Three Behrs may be reached at:

Three Behrs
RD # 8 Horsepound Road
Carmel, NY 10512
(914) 225-4747

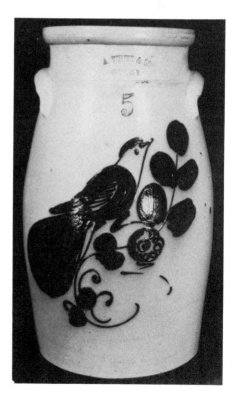

Five-gallon churn signed "N. A. White & Son, Utica, N.Y." with huge cobalt paddle-tail bird, restored condition. **$1450–$1550**

Three-gallon straight-sided crock signed "F. B. Norton & Co., Worcester, Mass.," in need of repair to a crack. **$150–$160**

Stoneware bottle signed "BF and CC Haley/California Pop Beer 1895," 9½″ tall. **$65**

One-gallon ovoid jar, signed "N. White, Utica." **$150–$160**

Three-gallon wide-mouthed jar signed "N. C. Bell/Kingston," 3″. **$500–$550**

Stoneware barrel with "USA" stamped on the bottom, unglazed and molded, 6½″ tall, **$20–$30;** stoneware barrel, unmarked, 7″ tall, **$20–$30.**

Three-gallon churn signed "E. and L. P. Norton, Bennington, Vt." **$750–$825**

Four-gallon jug-cooler signed "W. H. Farrar & Co., Geddes, N.Y." **$4400–$4600**

One-gallon unmarked Pennsylvania pitcher with brushed deocration. **$700–$750**

Four-gallon straight-sided crock signed "C. Hart and Son, Sherburne" (N.Y.). **$250–$350**

One-gallon Pennsylvania pitcher, unmarked, 11" tall. **$700-$750**

Seven-gallon storage jar signed "Hamilton and Jones, Star Potter, Greensboro, Pa." **$800-$1000**

Three-gallon jug signed "Geddes, N.Y." with slip-trailed blossoms. **$175-$200**

Two-quart wax sealer preserve jar, 9" tall, c. 1870. **$230-$250**

Three-gallon jug signed "Frank B. Norton, Worcester, Mass." 15″ tall, c. 1879. **$750–$800**

One-gallon batter pail, signed "Cowden and Wilcox, Harrisburg," 9″ tall, c. 1872. **$1900–$2100**

Four-gallon straight-sided crock signed "N. A. White and Son, Utica, N.Y." with urn or compote holding two flowers, 12″ tall, c. 1884. **$650–$700**

Another angle of the one-gallon batter pail.

Three-gallon jar signed "Bremer and Halm, Havana, N.Y." **$585–$615**

Three-gallon wide-mouth jar signed "C. Crolius/Manufacturer/Manhattan Wells/ New York." **$2000–$3000**

One-gallon crock signed "New York Stoneware Co." with floral cobalt decoration. **$200–$250**

Three-gallon crock signed "W. Roberts, Binghampton, N.Y." **$700–$750**

Two-gallon jar signed "Whites, Utica, N.Y." with slip-trailed chicken or rooster. **$300–$400**

Four-gallon ovoid jug signed "N. Clark and Co., Lyons, N.Y."**$700–$800**

Three-gallon jar signed "Pottery Works, N.Y.," c. 1866. **$2400–$2600**

One-and-one-half-gallon batter pail signed "Cowden and Wilcox" with cobalt leaves and berries. **$2800–$3000**

119

Two-gallon milk pan signed "Lyons," 6½" tall, c. 1860. **$1700–$1800**

Ovoid jar with lid signed "L. Norton and Son," c. 1835, with cobalt moth or butterfly. **$1400–$1600**

Four-gallon jug signed "Whites Utica," 18" tall, with running bird. **$1100–$1300**

Five-gallon crock signed "West Troy Pottery," 13" tall, c. 1879. **$700–$800**

Three-gallon jar signed Leathers & Brother, Howard, Pa.," 12" tall. **$750–$800**

Two-gallon ovoid jar signed "Cowden and Wilcox, Harrisburg, Pa.," 10" tall, c. 1869. **$600–$700**

Four-gallon crock, unmarked, 12" tall, with minor restoration and "chicken pecking corn" decoration. **$500–$600**

Four-gallon crock signed "Ottman Bros, Fort Edward, N.Y.," 12" tall, c. 1872. **$475–$500**

Two-gallon crock signed "Evan R. Jones, Pittston, Pa.," 9½" tall, c. 1879, with some glaze flaking. **$140–$175**

Three-gallon crock signed "E. and L. P. Norton, Bennington, Vt.," 10½" tall, c. 1871, with some rim chips. **$375–$425**

Two-gallon crock signed "John Burger, Rochester," c. 1861. **$1000–$1200**

Three-gallon jar signed "Ithaca, N.Y.," 12½" tall, c. 1886, with double flower. **$300–$375**

One-gallon Pennsylvania butter crock, unmarked, no lid, 5" tall, c. 1860. **$200–$225**

Two-gallon Pennsylvania pitcher signed "Sipe, Nichols, & Co., Williamsport, Pa.," 13" tall, c. 1872. **$1100–$1300**

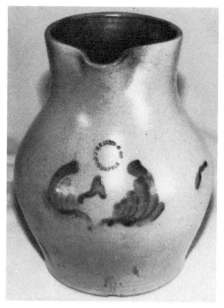

Two-gallon pitcher signed "J. B. Caire & Co.," 12" tall, c. 1842. **$2000–$3000**

Two-gallon ovoid Pennsylvania preserve jar signed "A. Conrad & Co., New Geneva, Pa.," 10" tall, c. 1872, with minor restoration. **$200–$225**

Three-gallon crock signed Evan R. Jones, Pittston, Pa.," 11" tall, c. 1870. **$1100–$1300**

123

One-gallon pitcher signed "West Troy Pottery," c. 1865. **$800–$850**

One-gallon milk pan signed "N. Clark & Co., Lyons," 5½" tall × 10" wide, c. 1837. **$1800–$1900**

Batter pail with stenciled decoration, 1½ gallon, F. H. Cowden, Harrisburg, Pa., 11" tall. **$1500–$1600**

One-gallon Pennsylvania pitcher, unmarked, 12" tall, c. 1860. **$625–$700**

Rare bell-shaped stoneware bank, unmarked, c. 1850. **$200–$250**

One-half gallon unmarked pitcher, probably made by the Robinson Clay Pottery Co. of Akron, Ohio, 8½″ tall, c. 1910. **$200–$250**

Three-gallon wide-mouth jar signed "M. Meade & Co.," 12″ tall. **$225–$250**

Four-gallon unmarked wide-mouthed jar, 13½″ tall, c. 1841. **$375–$450**

Pennsylvania preserve jar signed "Jas. Hamilton & Co., Greensboro, Pa." with stenciled fan and three broad stripes. **$275–$325**

Stoneware coffee pot, of approximately one-quart capacity, Bodine Pottery Co., Zanesville, Ohio, with tinware straps, handle, spout, cover, and wire bail handle all original and intact, $8\frac{1}{2}''$ tall, c. 1880. **$750–$825**

Three-gallon unmarked Pennsylvania butter crock with lid, 7" tall, c. 1860. **$750–$850**

One-gallon unmarked batter pail, probably Whites Pottery, Utica, N.Y., $9\frac{1}{2}''$ tall, c. 1860. **$1500–$1600**

Five-gallon jug signed "W. Roberts, Binghamton, N.Y.," some base chips, 20" tall, c. 1874. **$550–$650**

One-gallon unmarked batter pail, 10½″ tall, c. 1875. **$400–$460**

Stoneware bottle, one pint, unmarked, 8½″ tall, c. 1860. **$200–$225**

Three-quart Pennsylvania preserve jar, unmarked vendor's jar from Wheeling W. Va., 10″ tall, c. 1865. **$250–$300**

Three-gallon straight-sided crock signed "West Troy, N.Y., Pottery," extensively restored, 11″ tall, c. 1879. **$2000–$3000**

Mug made by Whites Pottery, Utica, N.Y., 5½" tall, c. 1895. **$40–$50**

One-gallon spittoon signed "R. C. R., Phila." 5" tall, c. 1865. **$350–$450**

Mug made by Central New York Pottery, Utica, N.Y., 5" tall, c. 1894, **$125–$175;** mug made by Central New York Pottery, with restored lip chip, 5" tall, **$125–$135.**

Two-gallon jar made by O. L. and A. K. Ballard, Burlington, Vt., 11" tall, c. 1862. **$300–$400**

Unmarked flask, $8\frac{1}{2}''$ tall, c. 1895. $115–$140

One-gallon batter pail, unmarked with chips around spout and rim, 9" tall, c. 1865. $115–$130

Five-gallon crock made by Whites, Utica, N.Y., 13" tall, c. 1862. $550–$600

Two-gallon jar signed "Norton & Fenton, Bennington, Vt.," 11" tall, c. 1844. $550–$600

One-gallon unmarked harvest jug of questionable age, 15″ tall. **$175–$200**

Three-gallon unmarked barrel cooler, 14½″ tall, c. 1867. **$450–$550**

Six-gallon straight-sided crock signed "Fort Edward Stoneware, Co.," c. 1885. This is a "puzzle" crock with six birds hidden in the decoration. **$2100–$2400**

Three-gallon straight-sided crock signed "C. W. Braun, Buffalo, N.Y." with "leaping leopard" cobalt decoration, 10½″ tall, c. 1870. **$3400–$3600**

Three-gallon straight-sided crock signed "J. Burger Jr., Rochester, N.Y." and "1889" with minor rim chips and some glaze flaking, 10″ tall. **$300–$400**

Two-gallon jug signed "West Troy, N.Y. Pottery," 15″ tall, c. 1879. **$750–$850**

One-gallon pitcher signed "Burger & Lang, Rochester, N.Y.," 10″ tall, c. 1870. **$1400–$1550**

Three-gallon straight-sided crock signed "J. & E. Norton, Bennington, Vt.," c. 1851. **$6900–$7100**

Old Sleepy Eye

Old Sleepy Eye (1780–1860) was a well-known Sioux Indian chief who lived in what is now Minnesota. Located in the town of Sleepy Eye, Minnesota, was a large flour mill that started business in 1883 as the Sleepy Eye Milling Company. The mill produced a variety of products that included flour, cereals, pancake flour, and a wheat-based coffee substitute.

The Sleepy Eye Milling Company closed in 1921. During its existence the mill created a large variety of advertising premiums carrying the picture of Chief Sleepy Eye that are in great demand among collectors today.

The best-known items are the stoneware premiums produced by the Weir Pottery Company of Monmouth, Illinois, from 1903 to 1906; and the Old Sleepy Eye Pottery manufactured by the Western Stoneware Company until 1937.

Molded steins, vases, salt bowls, and butter crocks were made in addition to five sizes of pitchers. The pitchers are found in half-pint, pint, quart, half-gallon, and gallon sizes.

Other items issued by the Sleepy Eye Milling Company included a chalkware match holder, bronze paperweights, 15″ wooden rulers, calendars, cookbooks, fans, china plates, trade cards, postcards, tin signs, flour sacks, stationery, trivets, and two sizes of stoneware mugs.

In 1976 a collectors club originated in Monmouth and held a convention, and today the club has more than one thousand members nationally. The club's purpose is to increase knowledge of Old Sleepy Eye collectibles through its quarterly newsletters and to provide a yearly convention for members to buy and sell related collectibles.

Information about membership in the club may be obtained by writing:

Old Sleepy Eye Collector's Club
P.O. Box 12
Monmouth, IL 61462

"Hummer" paper flour sack. **$300–$350**

Cloth flour sack. **$200–$250**

132

"That Sleepy Eye Flour" tin advertising sign. **$800–$1000**

"Cream" cloth flour sack. **$300–$350**

Flemish blue and gray stoneware vase. **$175–$225**

Blue and white stoneware trivet or hot plate. **$1800–$2200**

133

Flemish blue and gray stoneware butter crock. **$500–$600**

Chalkware match holder. **$500–$600**

Mug without a verse. **$1800–$2000**

Set of five blue on white pitchers: #1 through #4, **$150–$250;** #5, **$250–$350.**

Blue-rimmed half-gallon pitcher. **$350–$450**

Old Sleepy Eye pillow top. **$300–$400**

"Cream" barrel label. **$150–$200**

"Monroe" pillow top. **$250–$350**

"Chief" barrel label. **$150–$200**

1904 calendar. **$175–$250**

"Hummer" barrel label. **$250–$350**

Machine-dovetailed wooden packing box.
$350–$400

Clothespin apron. **$150–$200**

Bronze letter opener. **$300–$400**

Die-cut fan on a stick. **$100–$150**

5 *Evaluating Country Chairs*

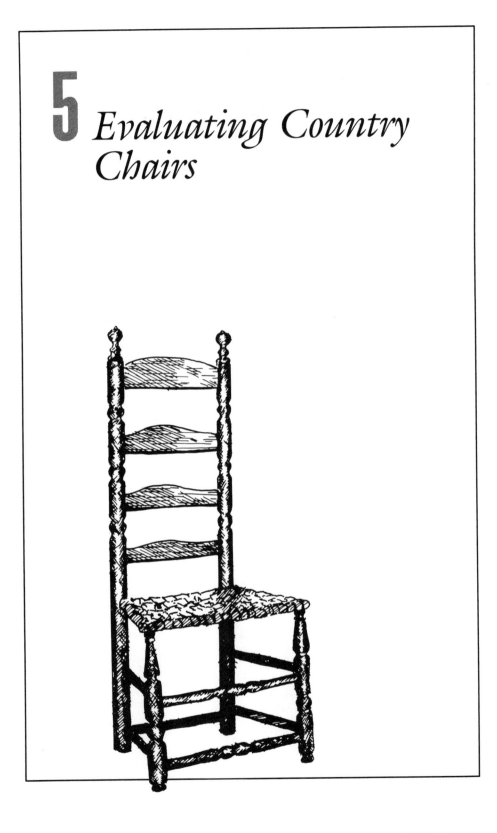

A variety of woods commonly was used in most country chairs, with each wood serving a specific purpose. The assortment of colors and grains used made little difference, because the chairs always were painted.

Many "simple" rocking chairs or side chairs are called Shaker chairs. The Shakers were in the rocking chair business for more than a century. After the early 1870s the chairs were mass-produced at Mount Lebanon, New York. The Shakers continued to make the same chairs until the early 1940s, when the factory burned.

Purchasing country chairs, or any other article of country furniture, requires that you do some homework ahead of time. For example, when the stretchers of a chair (or table) are within an inch of the floor, it is usually an excellent bet that the piece lost some of its leg height at some point. The

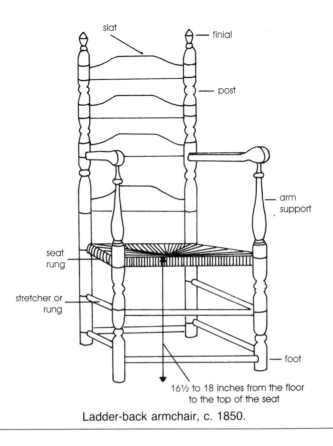

slat

finial

post

arm support

seat rung

stretcher or rung

foot

16½ to 18 inches from the floor to the top of the seat

Ladder-back armchair, c. 1850.

term "pieced out" means that several inches are added to a chair to give it back its original leg length. The most difficult part of piecing out a chair is matching the paint on the new sections of leg with the old paint on the remainder of the chair.

Before you write the next check for a country chair, study for following notes very carefully.

The top of a chair seat should be no less than 16½" to 18" from the floor.

Rocking chairs should be 14" to 16" from the floor to the top of the seat.

The legs on old chairs are oval ("out of round") rather than round because wood shrinks across the grain and turns a circle into an oval.

The lowest rung (stretcher) on a chair is usually the most worn from contact with heels and feet.

The upper chair rung is usually much less worn.

The finials on the chair posts also are out of round.

The back side of the chair finials should be worn smooth from coming in contact with a wall numerous times when the individual sitting in it leaned back.

The finials and the back posts should be turned from a single piece of wood.

The "front" of the chair feet should be worn smooth from the chair having been pulled across a floor.

The back feet should be equally as worn.

140

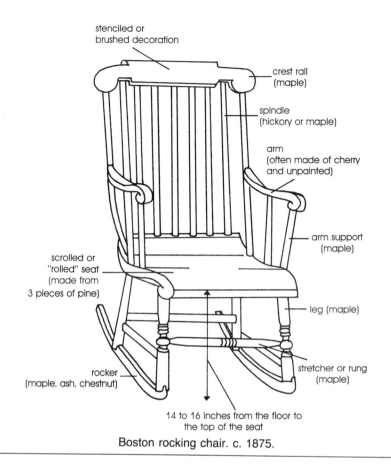

stenciled or
brushed decoration

crest rail
(maple)

spindle
(hickory or maple)

arm
(often made of cherry
and unpainted)

arm support
(maple)

scrolled or
"rolled" seat
(made from
3 pieces of pine)

leg (maple)

rocker
(maple, ash, chestnut)

stretcher or rung
(maple)

14 to 16 inches from the floor to
the top of the seat

Boston rocking chair. c. 1875.

The seats of most chairs (other than Boston rockers) should be made from a single piece of thick pine.

The underside of the seat should not be painted.

The "paint history" of the chair may be read by studying the underside of the seat, where paint brushes came in contact with the top of the legs each time the chair was painted.

The chair's rungs (stretchers) should have almost identical shape, thickness, and "paint history."

The stretchers should be equally out of round or oval.

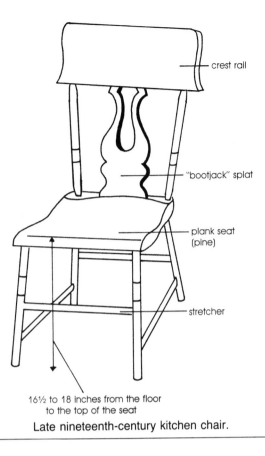

crest rail

"bootjack" splat

plank seat (pine)

stretcher

16½ to 18 inches from the floor
to the top of the seat

Late nineteenth-century kitchen chair.

James D. Julia, Inc.

Eighteenth-century sack-back Windsor armchair with bowed back, shaped hand rest, scooped-out seat, bulbous turned legs and stretchers, and black paint over an earlier coat of black paint, **$1400**; eighteenth-century sack-back armchair with bulbous turned base and stretchers, nicely turned bulbous arm supports, and paint that is either original or a very early overpaint, **$2600**.

Eighteenth-century ladder-back rocker with four-slat back, turned posts and rolled arms, stenciled slats with old red overpaint, and replaced rush seat. **$625**

Eighteenth-century ladder-back side chair with very fine turned posts and finials and old black overpaint. **$500**

Set of four step-down decorated period Windsor side chairs. **$3400**

Chair table with block and turned legs with turned stretchers, top hinge is permanently fastened to base, curled or scrolled hand grips, and original red paint. **$2100**

Early twentieth-century settee signed "Wallace Nutting." **$1350**

Set of six Pennsylvania "half" spindle chairs. **$800**

Set of six Pennsylvania "bootjack" kitchen chairs. **$475**

Baltimore "fancy" chair. **$350**

Set of six nineteenth-century signed "Hitchcock" chairs. **$1650**

6 Antiques Malls, Cooperatives, and Group Shops

In the mid-1960s we went out in search of country antiques five nights a week. Every central Illinois hamlet and town had an antiques shop located in somebody's basement, back porch, or all over the house. Many of these shops advertised "general line" antiques—indicating that they offered carnival glass and dry sinks.

Many of the shops were operated by middle-aged ladies who received telephone calls when anything of consequence was for sale within a twenty-mile radius. They went to farm auctions, estate sales, and bought from "pickers" who stopped by for a piece of pie while passing through their town with a pickup truck full of antiques.

The hours in these shops were much more flexible than the prices. They offered dealer discounts to the "trade" but only advice to us.

We gradually learned what we liked and over time and thousands of miles built up some positive relationships and a growing collection of country antiques. In retrospect we actually have no regrets about anything we bought during that period. The only lingering concern is for what we failed to purchase due to a lack of knowledge or funding.

Since that time there have been major changes in the way antiques are marketed. The individual antiques shops have tended to become obscured by the growing number of "antiques" malls that have taken over every abandoned supermarket in North America.

Many of the malls are not worth your time because the owners are motivated primarily by filling the building with dealers and their pockets at the expense of the quality of the items offered for sale.

As we have noted in previous volumes of this book, there are some selected exceptions to this trend. There are antiques malls across the nation that maintain high standards of merchandise and closely monitor the quality of the dealers that they allow to occupy sapce.

These malls tend to specialize in a particular segment of antiques. The ones we favor lean aggressively toward Americana.

The cooperative or group shop concept is also a relatively recent development in many parts of the United States. In a cooperative or group shop, a limited number of dealers with similar interests and ranges of merchandise come together to sell antiques. They share operating and advertising costs and spend comparable amounts of time working in the business. They are familiar with the items for sale and typically can informatively answer questions that a customer may have about a particular piece. In the antiques mall down on the corner, where the grocery store used to be, this is the exception rather than the rule.

Midwest Country Antiques

Midwest Country Antiques is a group shop owned by Larry and Pat Coughlin and Darrell and Lana Potter. It is located between Terre Haute, Indiana, and St. Louis, Missouri, on I-70 in downtown St. Elmo, Illinois, an oil-boom town of the 1930s. The shop is open daily, Monday through Saturday, from 9 A.M. to 5 P.M. and on Sundays by appointment. The shop specializes in American country antiques.

Additional information may be obtained by contacting:

Darrell and Lana Potter
Rural Route 2
Box 193
St. Elmo, IL 62458
(618) 829-5471

Carved spoon rack. **$250**

Painted pine bench with horse. **$125**

Mustard painted pine wooden box with hinged lid. **$145**

Green painted spice chest with six drawers. **$325**

Painted pine bench. **$65**

Blue tool carrier with dovetailed ends. **$165**

Blue pine knife box, **$185;** small blue turned bowl, **$125.**

Painted blind-front cupboard from a mining shack in Witt, Illinois. **$1145**

Blue blanket box with peg construction. **$650**

Painted hanging cupboard. **$245**

Pine "mustard" jelly cupboard. **$525**

Walnut sugar chest with pegged construction. **$1195**

"Bill" the advertising dog. **$295**

Red and blue pine table. **$295**

Poll Parrot Shoe advertisement made of chalkware. **$210**

Trade sign. **$175**

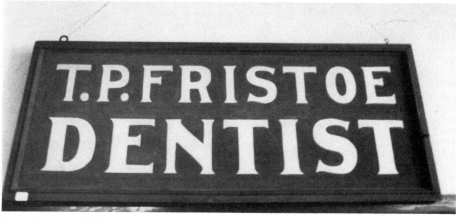

Dentist's sign. **$185**

Saint Nicholas plaque from New Orleans theater, 36" diameter, c. early 1900s. **$1200**

Weatherbird Shoes cloth advertising banner. **$50**

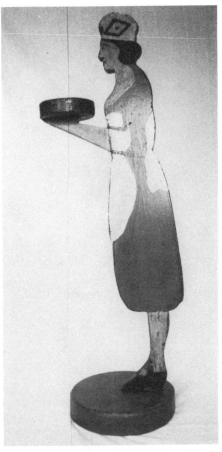

Folk art lady butler from a southern Illinois restaurant, c. 1930. **$135**

Salesman's sample copper wash boiler. **$235**

Painted boxes with drop handles. **$225** each

Bride's box with blue paint and initials "C.A. 1837." **$395**

Blue painted buttocks basket. **$325**

Oak splint baskets with colored splint detail. **$185** each

Footed cotton storage basket, painted white. **$185**

"Chicken coop" basket used for carrying roosters to cockfights. **$275**

Red painted splint basket. **$250**

156

Red painted maple bowl. **$165**

Mail coach from the 1930s, *Popular Mechanics* model. **$450**

Oak splint half basket. **$110**

Red folk art schoolhouse, c. 1930s. **$145**

Painted pine birdhouse, **$225**

158

White house with blue trim. **$225**

Red, white, and blue Teddy bear, **$695;** brown Teddy bear with movable arms and legs, **$350.**

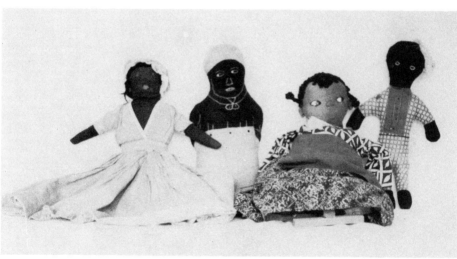

Black rag dolls. **$95–$125** each

Folk art child's tractor, c. 1940. **$75**

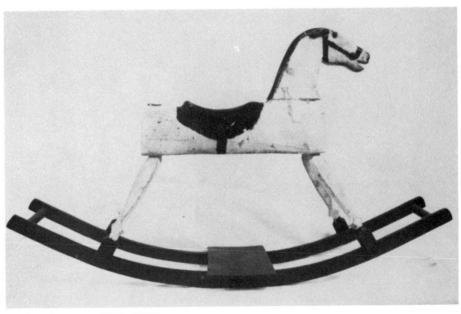

Rocking horse, c. 1900. **$795**

German wagon in original painted condition. **$295**

White leather cow pull toy, **$450;** papier-mâché cow pull toy, **$450.**

Elephant pull toy filled with straw. **$495**

161

Canvas goose decoy. **$175**

Rabbit pull toy. **$95**

Painted highchair. **$195**

162

Leather and wood saddle. **$95**

Wooden cat doorstop, c. 1930s. **$135**

"Hannah Jones" sampler with alphabet and numbers in red and green, nineteenth century. **$450**

Nineteenth-century oil painting. **$195**

Tole-painted tin coffeepot with carefully done oak graining. **$225**

Country Village Antiques

Country Village Antiques of Glendora, California, is a cooperative shop owned by sixteen dealers who specialize in early American antiques. The "Village" contains four thousand square feet of country antiques in room settings. Glendora is twenty-five miles east of downtown Los Angeles.

The Country Village has a large open house in early November and one in June. Shop hours are 10 A.M. to 5 P.M. Monday through Saturday and 11 A.M. to 4 P.M. on the last Sunday of each month. The mailing address is:

Country Village Antiques
163 N. Glendora Avenue
Glendora, CA 91740
(818) 914-2542
(818) 914-6860

Blue and white spongeware pitcher and bowl, c. 1870. **$750**

Ironstone teapot, late nineteenth century. **$145**

Ferry seed box, oak, c. 1900. **$195**

Blue and white "tree of life" quilt, c. 1890. **$1500**

Restored American primitive painting by "Grandmother" H. Smith, Boston, Mass., vicinity, c. 1878. **$12,000**

Hooked rug with cottage scene, found in Maine, c. 1920. **$295**

"Running horse" hooked rug, New England, c. 1890. **$385**

Pine table with teal green paint, c. 1870-1900. **$395**

Connecticut trolley car megaphone, c. 1890, **$98;** child's gathering basket with white oak splint, **$350;** Pennsylvania one-half basket with oak splint, c. 1900; **$195**

Pine table with original painted finish. **$395**

Shaker berry buckets with original paint and small toy bucket, from left: **$275, $325, $40.**

166

Set of three cast-iron posnets, c. 1800s. **$335**

Painted pantry boxes, c. 1880. **$225–$275 each**

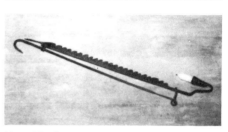

New England trammel candle holder, c. mid-eighteenth century. **$650**

Refinished pine pie safe, **$750;** Shaker oval pantry box with finger lap construction and late blue paint, **$495.**

Collection of sports equipment, c. 1920-1940. **$15–65**

New England maple and pine rope bed, c. 1860s. **$695**

Applique "coxcomb" quilt made by Pennsylvania Mennonites, c. 1900. **$900**

Wool coverlet with eagle border, dated 1849. **$950**

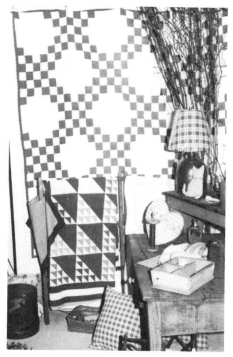

Red and white double Irish chain quilt, c. 1890. **$495**

Tin wall-hanging pie or dough "board" from Pennsylvania, c. 1900-1920. **$350**

Pine grain bin with old red paint, c. 1900. **$175**

Wrought-iron pot stand, c. 1890. **$65**

Hooked rug "basket of flowers" with scalloped border, c. 1870. **$395**

"Mammy" towel bar from Indiana, c. 1930. **$120**

Early mustard wall cupboard with square nail construction, c. 1860. **$1195**

Refinished pine dry sink, c. 1890. **$395**

Maple worktable, c. 1920, **$245;** pressed-back oak kitchen chairs, c. 1925, **$75** each.

Blue pine cupboard without its doors. **$525**

Refinished pine deacon's bench, 8' long. **$1195**

Tricycle in original condition with wooden handles and wire wheels, c. 1880–1890. **$550**

Midwestern pie safe with star tins and red and mustard paint, c. 1880. **$1095**

Early bear, **$550,** on handmade bed from the late nineteenth century, **$195.**

Papier-mâché horse pull toy on pine platform with original paint, c. 1860. **$250**

Old repaired Teddy bear, **$250;** mustard rocker, **$125;** blue pantry boxes, **$295** and **$245;** Amish doll, **$150.**

Express wagon with original painted finish of mustard and red, c. 1880–1910. **$750**

Shaker laundry basket. **$450**

Red painted doll bed with folding spindles, c. 1890. **$155**

Northeastern Indian basket with potato stamp decoration. **$195**

Blue carrier with leather strap, early twentieth century. **$90**

Log cabin, c. 1910. **$295**

Child's bucket, blue paint, 16″ diameter, nineteenth century. **$220**

Painted folk art windmill. **$175**

Red and green birdhouse from Pennsylvania. **$185**

173

Tin candlebox, c. 1850. **$350–$400**

Green teal Mason decoy, standard grade, tack eyes, c. 1895–1925. **$265**

Tin lantern, c. 1875. **$225**

Corn meal bin with original label, c. 1890–1910. **$295**

Sheet metal whirligig, Maine, twentieth century. **$795**

Blue painted gathering basket, nineteenth century, **$285;** uncut roll of flags with 42 stars, **$1600.**

Flannel baseball uniform, c. 1930. **$65**

Red, white and blue painted sign of pine with beardboard ends. **$495**

Lancaster Antiques Market

The Lancaster Antique Market is located in Lancaster, Kentucky, near Shakertown at Pleasant Hill. The mall contains more than twenty thousand square feet of Americana and is open from 10 A.M. to 5 P.M. Mondays through Saturdays and from 1 P.M. to 5 P.M. on Sundays. For a fee of $10, the Lancaster Antique Market offers a narrated videotape of items that currently are for sale (the fee is refundable with a purchase). Antiques are shipped daily via United Parcel Service (UPS) and freight.

Rose Holtzclaw and Ellen Tatem, owners of the market, also have a restored nineteenth-century bed and breakfast furnished with antiques that is used by visiting dealers and collectors. The address is:

Lancaster Antiques Market
102 Hamilton Avenue
Lancaster, KY 40444
(606) 792-4536

Pine chimney cupboard in putty color paint. **$2250**

Wood box-cupboard in gray paint, c. 1900. **$1495**

Small stand of drawers in brown paint. **$495**

Three long pine drawers in gray paint. **$150**

Painted pine bureau box with decorative inlay. **$125**

Dovetailed walnut candle box with lid. **$250**

Carrier with traces of salmon paint and drop handle. **$245**

Kentucky finely woven splint basket. **$295**

Unusual footed basket in red paint. **$295**

Staved sap bucket in red paint. **$50**

Apple box in original bittersweet paint. **$195**

177

Nineteenth-century hourglass. **$145**

Twig stand in green paint. **$50**

Early wooden and glazed candle lantern.
$350

Green quilt in excellent, original condition.
$750

Shaker picnic basket. **$195**

Blue and white ironstone platter. **$150**

Creekside Antiques

Creekside Antiques is located twenty minutes north of San Francisco, California, in the small community of San Anselmo. San Anselmo offers visitors more than 120 dealers offering a wide variety of antiques. Creekside Antiques is a cooperative or group shop with fifteen dealers who specialize in Americana, country furniture, pottery, and early textiles. The shop was the inspiration of Pat Newsom, who opened the business in 1988. You may contact Pat at:

Creekside Antiques
241 Sir Francis Drake
San Anselmo, CA 94960
(415) 457-1266

Cherry pie safe, c. 1840. **$1400**

Refinished pine Pennsylvania kas (Dutch cupboard or wardrobe), c. 1830. **$2000**

179

Pine dry sink with mustard paint, c. 1860.
$1400

Grain-painted pine cupboard, c. 1880.
$1400

Maple Sheraton chest of drawers with cookie cutter top, c. 1810–1820. **$2200**

Blue painted pine cupboard, c. 1840. **$3000**

Refinished pine step-back cupboard, c. 1860. **$1800**

Pine step-back cupboard. **$1400**

Refinished pine cricket table with scalloped trim, **$800**; pair of Windsor side chairs, **$700**.

Sheraton side table with flame-painted drawer. **$525**

Signed Hitchcock chair. **$275**

Pine chair table, c. 1850. **$1800**

Another view of the pine chair.

Early Hepplewhite country table with original red paint. **$1100**

Refinished maple and pine nineteenth-century settee. **$650**

Child's Boston rocking chair with painted finish, c. 1850. **$250**

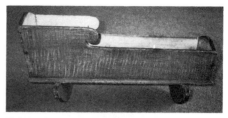

Original grain-painted doll cradle with square nail construction. **$235**

Composition Knickbocker Donald Duck, **$800;** Steiff Mickey Mouse, **$2000;** Lenci Donald Duck, **$450**

Horse and cart pull toy, c. early 1900s. **$495**

Ohio ladder-back rocking chair with rush seat, mid-nineteenth century. **$800**

Victorian comb box with applied hearts and stars. **$210**

Casey Jones pedal car, c. 1940. **$600**

"Blazing Stars" quilt with sawtooth borders, Michigan, c. 1880. **$3400**

Shaker-type sewing box from Maine, c. 1870s. **$265**

Carved folk art rooster. **$600**

Pennsylvania wall box, c. 1840. **$395**

Spongeware pitcher with raised design, c. 1860. **$195**

Nineteenth-century copper teakettles signed by their maker: left, **$1200;** right, **$495.**

Cobalt-decorated stoneware, left to right: **$325, $300, $185.**

Sponge-decorated pitcher with cobalt bank, late nineteenth century. **$425**

Cobalt-decorated stoneware jug signed "F. H. Cowden, Harrisburg, Pa.," c. 1860s. **$395**

Nineteenth-century andirons. **$650**

Painted decoy by unknown carver, **$395;** "broadbill" drake carved by Doug Jester of Chincoteague, Va., c. 1920–1940, **$450.**

Early whale oil lamp. **$395**

Plaster store display piece, c. 1900. **$1800**

Tin anniversary hat, c. late nineteenth century. **$650**

Late nineteenth-century "tinsel" picture. **$395**

7 Collecting Antiques in the Midwest

This section was prepared by Shirley Dukes, who, with her husband, Ralph, operates Century House Antiques at 11 E. 2nd Street in El Paso, IL 61738. They have been in the antiques business for many years and do shows throughout the Midwest. They specialize in Americana.

Illinois, Wisconsin, and Iowa were largely populated after the Civil War. Land grants stimulated the move from the East to the Midwest. Many of these settlers arrived on trains rather than covered wagons. Most of their belongings were carried in carpetbags, trunks, and suitcases. Relatively few families were able to bring the furnishings of their previous residences with them due to the excessive cost of transportation.

Many midwestern homes are typically late Victorian, bungalow, or two-story structures with a front porch in the "prairie house" style. Some houses in the first quarter of the twentieth century were purchased in pieces or kits from the Sears and Roebuck catalog. Oak woodwork and built-in cupboards were popular.

There is no question that oak furniture is still plentiful in the Midwest because it was readily available through the great mail-order houses of Chicago and the prolific factories of Grand Rapids, Michigan.

Individuals who are interested in preserving homes from the last quarter of the nineteenth century and the early twentieth century are looking for furniture appropriate to the style of their homes. Mission oak, late Victorian walnut, and refinished oak from Grand Rapids are eagerly collected.

These furniture styles are available to midwestern collectors from auctions, antiques shows, malls, tag sales, and even yard sales.

Those who favor early American country antiques of superior quality are forced to look extra hard to fulfill their collecting desires. As noted previously, not a great deal of pre-Civil War furniture was brought to Illinois and Iowa. Most of the furniture was purchased or made after that period.

Kentucky, Indiana, and Ohio were settled earlier than Ilinois, Wisconsin, and Iowa, and collectors historically have had an easier path to success in those states when searching for furnishings from 1820 to 1860.

Auctions

As people replaced their first generation "make-do" and hand-me-down, locally made furniture with Grand Rapids oak, the old stuff usually went to the barn or an out building. There it remained for several generations until the descendants decided to sell the estate. Many owners still tend to belittle the stuff out in the barn and are likely to burn it up or call a disposal service to haul it away.

I have some wonderful rag rugs that were literally pulled from a fire. These were saved. Too bad I was too late for the rest.

In central Illinois we are experiencing a period of auction fever, with many small and rural communities having a local auction on Wednesday or Friday evenings and a "town sale" one spring day each year. Regional antiques newspapers such as *The Collector* from Heyworth, Illinois, provide local information for individuals interested in journeying to the area.

A basic piece of advice for attending midwestern auctions is to dress for the worst possible weather if the auction is scheduled to be held outside.

Antiques Shows

Many of the Midwest's best examples of country furniture turn up at the numerous antiques shows held each weekend throughout Illinois, Wisconsin, Indiana, and Iowa. A copy of *Antique Week*, *The Collector*, or *Antique Trader* carry detailed advertisements and listings of these shows.

There are also a series of smaller, local shows held in rural grade school gymnasiums or township halls each spring that may have only fifteen or twenty dealers. On occasion some exceptional pieces of country furniture appear at these shows at reasonable prices.

190

Antiques Malls

Almost every midwestern community that contains a post office probably has at least two antiques malls, one of which is filled with garage sale leftovers, locally made crafts, and a clerk who knows what the "special" is at the restaurant on the corner but nothing about antiques.

The other mall in town can be well worth your time if the manager has maintained a degree of quality control and recruited dealers who offer carefully selected merchandise.

Antiques Shops

No, they are not dinosaurs—yet. Antiques shops are also "all over the map" in quality. Unlike antiques malls, the owner of the shop is usually on the premises to answer questions or discuss prices.

Many independent antiques shops can't afford the high-rent districts, so you often will find them outside of high-traffic areas. They are generally off the beaten track in somebody's basement, barn, garage, machine shed, or storefront. You need to seek them out—and the effort often is worth-while. You will find some wonderful items attractively displayed in the most unlikely places. You also will meet some of the most interesting people with significant antiques knowledge to share.

Buy a copy of Antique Week's Antique Shop Guide, complete with maps and shop listings, and hit the road.

Always ask antiques dealers about other shops in the immediate area. Most will gladly share information about locating other dealers. Good dealers are almost everywhere.

Walnut nightstand with one drawer, late nineteenth century. **$300–$400**

Child's wheelbarrow, found in Maine, with remnants of blue paint over red paint. **$175–$200**

Walnut jelly cupboard from New York State with all-pinned construction and red milk paint. **$900–$1200**

Refinished Victorian pine washstand. **$300–$400**

Line dryer, often incorrectly called a yarn winder, from Maine. **$65–$75**

Fishermen made these to dry their lines after a day of fishing.

Arts and Crafts era glass painted yellow and black. **$40–$60**

Pine doll cradle in original finish. **$125–$175**

Wicker feather ticket basket that holds one feather tick, 22" × 19" × 30". **$150–$200**

English Wedgwood and Copeland jelly molds. **$50–$85** each

Collapsible picnic basket signed "Duplex Folding Pail Co., York, U.S.A." in steel and brown canvas. **$50–$65**

Large tin cup and small pail with a wire bale handle. **$15–$25** each

American tin chamber sticks with push ups. **$50–$75** each

Pyrography picture frame with wood-burned decorations, 12" × 14". **$75**

Three-gallon Midwestern butter churn, unmarked, late nineteenth or early twentieth century, with Albany slip glaze. **$75–$95**

Tin muffin and cake molds, early 1900s. **$15–$25 each**

Double "betty" wrought-iron and sheet-iron grease lamp with eagles, rare, probably European in origin. **$150–$250**

Tin food molds, some of which are marked "Germany." The large cornucopia (at left) has original green paint. **$25–$35 each**

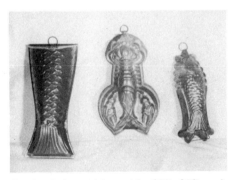

Seafood-shaped tin molds. **$30–$95 each**

Brass chamber stick with touch mark, c. eighteenth century. **$150–$200**

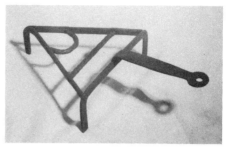

Hearth trivet c. eighteenth century. **$100–$200**

Brass candlestick with pushup, probably English. **$65–$75**

Early pine trunk with handwrought hardware, banding, and blue over red paint. **$400–$500**

"Rattletraps" used at chivarees to keep newlyweds awake with their popping sounds. **$50–$75 each**

Cherry chest of drawers with four drawers, original pulls, dovetailed drawers; feather-grained in original condition. **$600–$900**

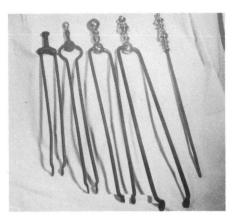

Early hearth tools, including iron and brass tongs and poker, eighteenth century. **$25–$95** each

Dutch wrought-iron crown meat hooks that hung from the trammel in the fireplace to cook game birds or meat chunks, eighteenth century. **$150–$200**

Tin roaster with punched lid, rare form, possibly a tenth anniversary gift, c. 1830–1860. **$175–$250**

Wrought-iron hearth spinner broiler, probably Shenandoah Valley origin, eighteenth century. **$150–$200**

Wrought-iron roasting grill, nicely embellished with hot twist on grids and handles, eighteenth century. **$150–$250**

8 *Country Store Collectibles*

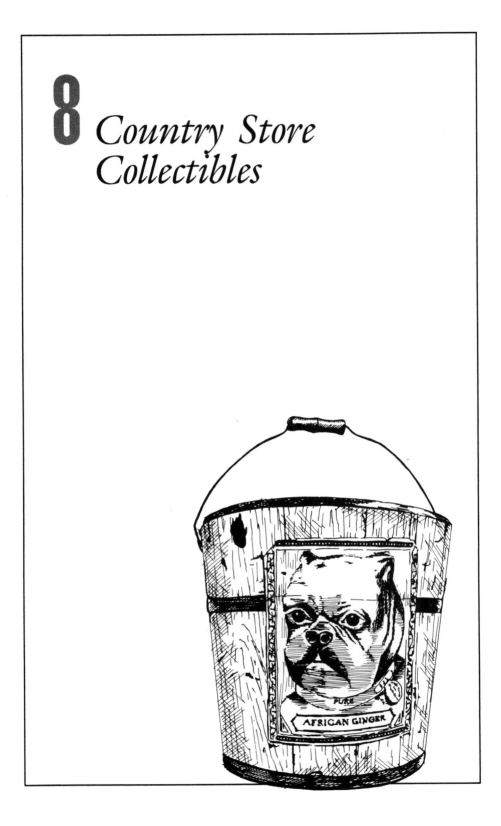

Old Storefront Antiques

Old Storefront Antiques specializes in country store items, pharmaceutical antiques, and collectible advertising. The Old Storefront offers eighteen general catalogs of merchandise for sale by mail, priced at $1.50 each or $25 for all eighteen. A listing of the catalogs according to subject (tins, soda fountain, pharmaceutical, and so forth) is available by sending a self-addressed stamped envelope to:

Patricia McDaniel
Old Storefront Antiques
P. O. Box 357
Dublin, IN 47335
(317) 478-4809

Abbott's cream cheese cardboard box (small). **$15**

Royal Scarlet Macaroni box. **$5**

Home-Canners' Jar Rubbers. **$4** each

Duff's Layer Cake Mix. **$7.50**

Jack Sprat Cherry Preserves. **$20**

Canning jar rubbers: Top Flite, **$3.50**; Bull Dog, **$12.**

Nestle's one-gallon Chocolate Flavor Syrup container. **$10**

None So Good Butter Sweets candy display box. **$75**

Butter Stretcher Wafers. **$6**

Jack Frost Cinnamon and Sugar. **$23**

Great Seal imitation banana flavoring. **$35**

Fiberboard African Ginger container. **$275**

Edgar's Household Confectioner's Mixture.
$12

Crystal Peppo. **$3.50**

Wilsnap Lingerie Clasp. **$5**

Hoosier Poet Cloves. **$3.50**

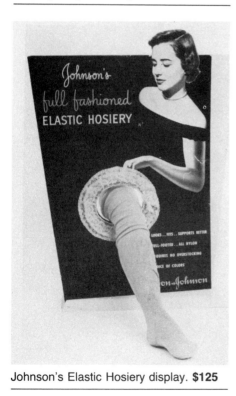

Johnson's Elastic Hosiery display. **$125**

Snow facial depilatory. **$40**

Klein's Japanese Cough Drops. **$15**

Putnam Soap Tints, **$3.50** each; display box, **$8.**

Fairies ironing starch. **$40**

Assorted razor blade packets: Keen Kutter Double Edge, **$5;** Gillette, **$2.75;** Monogram, **$4;** Probak, **$3.25;** Valet Auto-Strop, **$4.25;** Diamond Edge, **$3.75;** Gold Tone, **$4;** Segal, **$4.**

Ban-Smoke Chewing Gum. **$5.50**

Pain-A-Lay antiseptic. **$8**

Mother Goose shoe box. **$10**

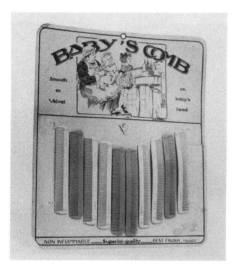

Baby's Comb complete display. **$40**

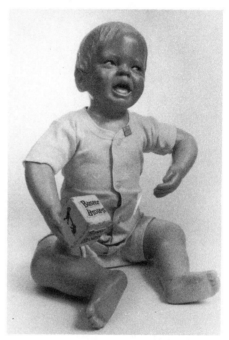

Buster Brown mannequin. **$175**

Culver Cubs white baby shoes. **$25**

Kenworthy's Cut-Out Letters. **$5**

Dyanshine Stove Polish. **$10**

ABC cards. **$9**

Semdac Liquid Gloss polish. **$15**

Clean Wall Cleaner. **$3.50**

Wet-Me-Wet glass and silver cleaner. **$7**

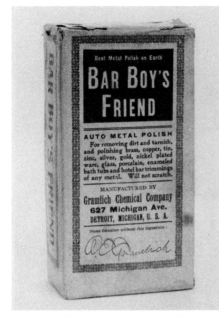

Bar Boy's Friend auto metal polish. **$7**

Nu-Bowl toilet bowl cleaner. **$5**

"Cool Off" Richardson's Freeze glass. **$25**

Soft drink bottles: Get Up, **$5.50**; Hermann, **$12**; Bubble Up, **$4.75**.

207

Primitive handmade wooden store display piece. **$65**

Ironhose advertisement. **$15**

Pop-Ade advertising sign. **$75**

Boye metal display piece for knitting needles. **$40**

Hickory Elastic store display case. **$200**

Hutton's Pork advertising pig. **$145**

Fluffy Pancakes and Bacon advertisement.
$15

Paper time clock store sign. **$10**

Mower's Pure Spruce Gum advertisement.
$27

Sunkist Oranges price calculator. **$7**

Superior Dog Biscuit box. **$10**

Paperweights: Georgia Department of Labor, **$14**; Western Grocer Co. Mills, **$45.**

Whoopee Song Restorer and Health Food. **$14**

Helena and West Helena, Arkansas, telephone book. **$10**

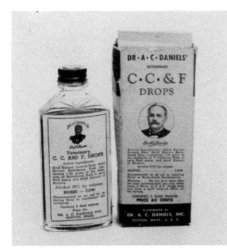

Dr. A. C. Daniels' CC & F Drops. **$15**

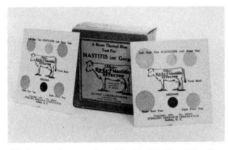

Globe Laboratories Ko-Ex-7 Mastitis Detector. **$10**

Blosser's Medical Powder. **$15**

Dr. Hess Medicated Powder. **$15**

Dr. David Roberts' Physic Balls horse medicine. **$10**

Hero Fire Extinguishers. **$12** each

Spratt's Insect and Flea Powder. **$15**

Gopher Corn poison. **$15**

Hammond's Slug Shot pesticide. **$12**

Acme London Purple insecticide. **$15**

Den Smokers pesticide. **$8**

Service station items: cardboard gas price sign, **$3.75;** "Contains Lead" sign, **$20**

Alligator Steel Belt Lacing. **$18**

Mobil tire tube. **$15**

Liquid Thread mending paste. **$10**

Carter's Ink. **$6**

Triangle Chalk. **$2** each

The Boss Patent Hook Huskers, **$13** each; display box, **$8.**

Souvenir decals. **$3.25** each

De-Linter Brush. **$9**

Genuine Nails, **$8** each; display box, **$5.**

Spalding's Club Practice Shuttlecocks. **$10**

Whirl-O-Halloween Fortune and Stunt Game card. **$25**

Charlotte M. Haines seed catalog, 1937. **$12**

Markley's African Violet Plant Food. **$7**

Wagner Ware metal display rack for self-basting covers. **$125**

Meyer and Faehr wooden cigar box. **$15**

Polar Ice Chopper. **$22**

Tissue Roping. **$13**

Brilliant Aluminum Wreath. **$17**

Final Examination

This is the eleventh final examination that we have put together to test your knowledge of American country antiques. We have spent more than an hour preparing this ultimately intellectual challenge especially for you.

The recognition that we have recently received from the National Association of Plasterers has been most gratifying for us and is sincerely appreciated.

Several of our earlier examinations are being used as entrance requirements at a school of animal husbandry in Iowa and at a clinic for chronic bad-check writers in Erie, Pennsylvania.

Each question has been tested on a random group of country antiques collectors. Those that could read did surprisingly well. Several of those who did less well have recently joined forces to open their own chain of antiques appraisal services.

Directions

1. Read each question carefully.

2. If you do not understand the question, raise your hand and someone will probably get to you.

3. Do not linger.

4. Usually, there is only one correct response.

5. If you are a veteran of Shays' Rebellion or San Juan Hill, you automatically receive five bonus points. If you attended elementary school with Daniel Shays or Juan Hill, you automatically receive two additional bonus points.

6. Your score will be posted on Thursday, next week, or in August.

Questions

1. Who said "Most antiques shows are like church; many attend but few understand"?
   a. Kazimierz Pulaski
   b. Leo Gorcey
   c. Leo Durocher
   d. none of the above

2. This dry sink dates from approximately
   a. 1850–1875
   b. 1880–1915
   c. after 1930
   d. none of the above

3. It appears to be made of walnut.
   true   false

4. This sink is worth approximately
   a. less than $250
   b. less than $500
   c. more than $600
   d. more than $750

5. The color that would add the *most* to the value of the sink is
   a. white
   b. black
   c. purple
   d. yellow

6. The front of the sink is made of wainscoting.
   true   false

7. This is a piece of country furniture.
   true   false

8. It dates from approximately
   a. 1820   c. 1920
   b. 1875   d. 1940

9. It appears to be made of pine.
   true   false

10. This piece is worth
    a. less than $200
    b. more than $200 but less than $375
    c. less than $100
    d. more than $400

11. This dry sink appears to be made of
    a. walnut
    b. oak
    c. maple
    d. pine

12. This painted sink is worth approximately
    a. less than $300
    b. more than $500 but less than $1000
    c. more than $1500 but less than $1800
    d. more than $2000

13. The value of the sink would be enhanced if the paint was removed.
    true   false

14. The fact that the drawer is on the left side diminishes the value of the sink.
    true   false

15. This pie safe appears to have been made of a combination of oak and ash.

    true   false

16. The value would be enhanced if the pierced tins on the doors had been replaced at some point with screen wire.

    true   false

17. This pie safe dates from approximately

    a. 1820–1830
    b. 1860–1880
    c. 1890–1910
    d. prior to 1820

18. The approximate value of this pie safe is more than $600.

    true   false

19. Check the statements below that are *true*.

    _____ Most pie safes are made of walnut.

    _____ A mahogany pie safe would be considered "rare."

    _____ Copper was often used in the doors in place of tin.

    _____ Screen wire panels are "later" than pierced tins.

    _____ A blue pie safe is typically worth more than one of comparable condition in red paint.

    _____ A green pie safe is typically worth more than one of comparable condition in brown paint.

    _____ A pine pie cupboard with brown paint and American eagles pierced in the tin panels on the doors is worth *at least* $1300.

    _____ There are more pie safes found today in Utah and Idaho than in Indiana and Pennsylvania.

20. "Sleepy Eye" stoneware was made at the Monmouth Pottery, Monmouth, Illinois.

    true   false

21. This is a "Hummer" _____ _____.

22. It dates from about
    a. 1840   c. 1900
    b. 1870   d. 1940

23. Its current value is at least $200.
    true   false

24. This footstool appears to be made of
    a. oak
    b. walnut
    c. mahogany
    d. pine

25. Pieces like this stool are difficult to date because they were made in a similar fashion for more than 100 years.
    true   false

26. This stool has a value of *at least* $200.
    true   false

27. This painted carpenter's chest dates from about 1850.
    true   false

28. It is probably made of
    a. oak
    b. pine
    c. walnut
    d. combination of oak, ash, and pine

29. The basket is made of
    a. rush
    b. walnut splint
    c. pine splint
    d. oak splint

30. This cupboard was factory made.
    true   false

31. The value of this cupboard is approximately $250–$500.
    true   false

32. The tin panels on this cupboard have been removed and wooden panels were inserted.
    true   false

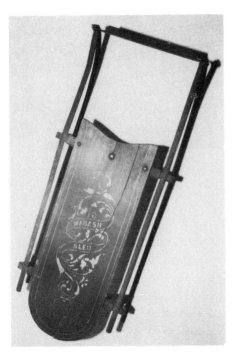

33. The decoration on this "Wabash Sled" was stenciled.
    true   false

34. The value of the sled would be enhanced if the paint was removed to show the grain of the wood.
    true   false

35. The sled dates from
    a. 1820–1830
    b. 1850–1870
    c. 1880–1910
    d. after 1930

36. The approximate value of the sled is
    a. $50–$75
    b. $150–$225
    c. $400–$500
    d. more than $500

37. This pitcher was probably *not* made in the United States.
    true   false

38. A pitcher like this example could be called a "noggin."
    true   false

39. This piece of furniture was factory made in the late nineteenth century.
    true   false

40. It appears to be made of walnut.
    true   false

41. The approximate value of this commode is
    a. $75–$125
    b. $200–$350
    c. $500–$650
    d. more than $650

42. If this basket was made in 1891 rather than 1991, it would be worth a minimum of $300.
    true   false

43. The value of the wheelbarrow is
    a. $75–$100
    b. $150–$200
    c. $225–$300
    d. more than $400

44. How much would a coat of seventy-five-year-old blue paint add to its value?
    a. less than $100
    b. more than $175

45. The Heart of Country Antiques Show is held each year in
    a. New Orleans
    b. Cleveland
    c. St. Louis
    d. none of the above

Optional Essay Question (10 points)

Points will be deducted for poor punctuation and relevant grammatical errors. Points will be added for positive references to Hector Gorch and his life and times.

Discuss in detail the rise and fall of Sylvester Klein's Used Furniture Emporium of Danville, Illinois. Do *not* mention his marital woes or his brother's phobic reaction to ice cubes in your answer.

Answers

1. d
2. a
3. false
4. b
5. d

6. true
7. false
8. c
9. false
10. a

11. a
12. b
13. false
14. false
15. false
16. false
17. b
18. true
19. A mahogany pie safe would be considered "rare."

   Screen wire is "later."

   A green pie safe is worth more.

   A pine pie cupboard (safe) with brown paint and eagles is worth more than $1800.
20. true
21. windmill weight
22. c
23. true
24. d

25. true
26. false
27. false
28. b
29. d
30. true
31. true
32. false
33. true
34. false
35. c
36. b
37. true
38. true
39. true
40. true
41. b
42. true
43. b
44. b
45. d

Scoring Scale

45–50 A scholarship will be established in perpetuity and your name will be held in reverence at Ralph's College, where they train transmission technicians.

40–44 The next time you are in Yuton, Illinois, you may redecorate any trailer in town. The only restriction on this premium is that the purple plastic curtains must remain on the premises. The shag carpet is negotiable.

35–39 A booth in an antiques mall of your choosing will be repiled in your honor.

less than 35 At the next local meeting of Low Achievers Anonymous, you will be given a special certificate in recognition of your years of service.